GALLUP YOUTH SURVEY:

MAJOR ISSUES AND TRENDS

TEENS & VOLUNTEERISM

Hal Marcovitz

Developed in Association with the Gallup Organization

TEENS & VOLUNTEERISM

Hal Marcovitz

**Developed in
Association with the
Gallup Organization**

Mason Crest
450 Parkway Drive, Suite D
Broomall, PA 19008
www.masoncrest.com

CPSIA Compliance Information: Batch #GYS2013. For further information, contact Mason Crest at 1-866-MCP-Book

First printing
1 3 5 7 9 8 6 4 2

Library of Congress Cataloging-in-Publication Data

    Marcovitz, Hal.
    Teens and volunteerism / Hal Marcovitz.
       pages cm. — (The Gallup youth survey : major issues and trends)
    Includes bibliographical references and index.
    Audience: Grade 7 to 8.
    ISBN 978-1-4222-2960-6 (hc)
    ISBN 978-1-4222-8877-1 (ebook)
    1. Teenage volunteers in social service — United States — Juvenile literature.
    2. Voluntarism — United States — Juvenile literature. I. Title.
    HN90.V64M36 2014
    302'.14 — dc23
                        2013007185

The Gallup Youth Survey: Major Issues and Trends series ISBN: 978-1-4222-2948-4

Contents

Introduction

By George Gallup

As the United States moves into the new century, there is a vital need for insight into what it means to be a young person in America. Today's teenagers will be the leaders and shapers of the 21st century. The future direction of the United States is being determined now in their hearts and minds and actions. Yet how much do we as a society know about this important segment of the U.S. populace who have the potential to lift our nation to new levels of achievement and social health?

We need to hear the voices of young people, and to help them better articulate their fears and their hopes. Our youth have much to share with their elders—is the older generation really listening? Is it carefully monitoring the hopes and fears of teenagers today? Failure to do so could result in severe social consequences.

The Gallup Youth Survey was conducted between 1977 and 2006 to help society meet this responsibility to youth, as well as to inform and guide our leaders by probing the social and economic attitudes and behaviors of young people. With theories abounding about the views, lifestyles, and values of adolescents, the Gallup Youth Survey, through regular scientific measurements of teens themselves, served as a sort of reality check.

Surveys reveal that the image of teens in the United States today is a negative one. Teens are frequently maligned, misunderstood, or simply ignored by their elders. Yet over four decades the Gallup Youth Survey provided ample evidence of the very special qualities of the nation's youngsters. In fact, if our society is less racist, less sexist, less polluted, and more peace loving, we can in considerable measure thank our young people, who have been on the leading edge on these issues. And the younger generation is not geared to greed: survey after survey has shown that teens have a keen interest in helping those people, especially in their own communities, who are less fortunate than themselves

Young people have told Gallup that they are enthusiastic about helping others, and are willing to work for world peace and a healthy world. They feel positive about their schools and even more positive about their teachers. A large majority of American teenagers have reported that they are happy and excited about the future, feel very close to their families, are likely to marry, want to have children, are satisfied with their personal lives, and desire to reach the top of their chosen careers.

But young adults face many threats, so parents, guardians, and concerned adults must commit themselves to do everything possible to help tomorrow's parents, citizens, and leaders avoid or overcome risky behaviors so that they can move into the future with greater hope and understanding.

The Gallup Organization is enthusiastic about this partnership with Mason Crest Publishers. Through carefully and clearly written books on a variety of vital topics dealing with teens, Gallup Youth Survey statistics are presented in a way that gives new depth and meaning to the data. The focus of these books is a practical one—to provide readers with the statistics and solid information that they need to understand and to deal with each important topic.

— — —

America's unique tradition of volunteerism will continue to undergird society in the years ahead, judging by survey findings on today's high school students. Thirteen million young people are currently engaged in some type of voluntary service, with the numbers having swelled markedly over the last decade and a half.

There is every reason to encourage volunteerism among young people, and for parents to model this activity. Youth who serve others on a regular basis are found to be happier about themselves, do better in school, and set the pace for other potential volunteers. And, if engaged in the early years, volunteerism becomes an integral part of one's life, to the great benefit of society.

Teens and Volunteerism provides the reader with important information and insights into volunteerism among young people and the U.S. population as a whole. It is a much-needed book in light of the fact that many social observers maintain volunteerism is the glue that keeps democracy together and is our best hope for the future.

Chapter One

Young volunteers help sort donated goods at a local food pantry. Studies have consistently shown that most young people are willing to donate their time and energy to charitable causes that they believe in.

A Devotion to Volunteerism

While many of their friends and class-mates spend Friday nights at the movies or attending parties, 16-year-old Laura and 14-year-old Tricia pull duty at the headquarters of Explorer Post 53 in Darien, Connecticut, which serves as the town's 24-hour ambulance and rescue squad. The two teenagers, as well as the other young members of the post, do not actually spend much time at the unit's home base. They spend most of their time in the back of an ambulance, responding to calls for help throughout Darien.

Laura and Tricia are typical members of the Post 53 ambulance and rescue squad, which is mostly staffed by teenagers. They gave up a lot of their free time becoming certified as emergency medical technicians so they could join the squad. Each of the girls had to undergo 50 hours of first-aid training. Next, they were put to work performing menial tasks around Post 53 for months before the other members felt confident enough to accept them into the squad. Only 15 new members are admitted each year to the Post 53 ambulance squad. The intense screening process is structured so that only the most dedicated teens win a place on the squad. After all, the teenage ambulance volunteers have helped deliver babies, performed cardiopulmonary resuscitation (CPR), administered first aid to people who have attempted suicide, and responded to car crash scenes with multiple victims. After being treated by the Post 53 teen volunteers for an allergic reaction to multiple bee stings, Catherine Garrish told a reporter for *Scholastic Choices* magazine, "You don't realize these are 17- and 18-year-olds; they're so professional."

For many American teenagers, a devotion to volunteerism is as much a part of their lives as school and MTV. They have been born into a society that values community service, and teens have responded by tutoring struggling students, raising money for cancer research by participating in walk-a-thons, cleaning up public parks on Saturday mornings, and pulling duty for the local ambulance corps on Friday nights. Young people in the United States readily volunteer their services with no expectation of a paycheck. The rewards they receive are much more significant. "Teens who volunteer increase their knowledge of the world and the problems that face it," said a 1996 report by Independent Sector, a Washington-based consortium of nonprofit organizations. "Volunteering affords teens both an opportunity to shape their communities and to receive lifelong benefits. Furthermore, formal and informal volunteer experiences during teen years increase the possibility of continued volunteering in adulthood. Teen volunteering provides positive experiences for youth, benefits society, and establishes a foundation for lifelong civic duty."

The Gallup Organization, a national public-opinion polling firm, provided information for the Independent Sector report, which was titled "America's Teenage Volunteers." Gallup has also studied the issue of teen volunteerism through the Gallup Youth Survey, a long-time project by the firm to assess the views of young people in the United States. The organization reported an uptick in volunteerism by teens in the last years of the 20th century and the first years of the 21st. In 1988, the Gallup Youth Survey determined that 24 percent of young people between the ages of 13 and 17 donated their time to charitable causes. Fifteen years later, the Gallup Youth Survey found that 31 percent of the 1,200 young people questioned in the poll donated their time to community service.

In the ensuing decade, however, the rate of teen volunteerism declined a bit. In 2012, according to the Bureau of Labor Statistics (BLS), 27.4 percent of Americans age 16–19 did volunteer work.

The BLS, like Gallup, defines volunteers as persons doing unpaid work through or for an organization. But teens often give of their time in less formal settings. Counting those who did unpaid work "with clubs, groups, their family alone, friends alone, or on their own" — in addition to those who did unpaid work for an established organization — the 2012 "DoSomething.org Index on Young People and Volunteering" found that 54.2 percent of young people had volunteered at least once in the previous year. (DoSomething.org is a nonprofit organization that promotes social change through youth action.) Other surveys that define volunteering broadly also find that about half of American teens have volunteered in recent years.

Who Volunteers?

The Gallup Youth Survey found that teenagers who were most

A young female volunteer helps an older woman prepare food for the needy at a church program in Illinois. Studies show that teenage girls are more likely to volunteer than teenage boys.

likely to devote themselves to community service did well academically—some 42 percent of high academic achievers said they volunteered. Also, teenagers whose parents had attended college were likely to volunteer. Just 24 percent of teenagers whose parents had not attended college were likely to perform community service, but that number jumped to 33 percent if a student had one parent who attended college, and 41 percent if both parents attended college. Finally, 41 percent of students who attended church regularly said they volunteered, while just 25 percent of students who did not attend church regularly said they were willing to donate their time.

Research has shown that if parents performed community service as teenagers, their children are likely to continue that tradition. "Volunteering is an activity most likely to be cultivated early in childhood and during early teenage years," indicated the Independent Sector report. "Adults who report volunteering in their youth are twice as likely to volunteer as adults. More than one out of three of all teenagers, six out of 10 volunteers, started volunteering by the age of 14."

There is a gender difference when it comes to volunteering. In 2012, according to the BLS, 29.8 percent of females age 16–19 volunteered; the rate for males in the same age group was 25.1 percent. Other studies have consistently shown that teenage girls are more likely than boys to participate in civic activities, vote, or become involved in political campaigns. "Although the reasons for these findings are not completely clear, researchers have found consistent ties between empathy, positive social behaviors, and civic engagement," reported Child Trends, a Washington-based nonprofit research organization, in a 2002 study. "It may be that parents and society socialize girls to be more empathetic and therefore more pro-social."

Teenagers face many issues as they make decisions about volunteering. On a national scale, young people have been encouraged to devote themselves to community service by joining AmeriCorps, a federal program that enables them to earn money for college while giving at least 10 months of their lives to volunteerism. The largest group of volunteers in the United States are those who join the military. Since the Vietnam War era, the armed services have been composed entirely of volunteers—both male and female.

Many school districts in the United States take devotion to volunteerism very seriously. Some schools require students to participate in local community service projects as a prerequisite for graduation; opponents of this practice question the value of forcing young people to do good deeds.

Many teens have found that volunteering can lead to social change. People who volunteer their time and talents to elect a political candidate hope to see genuine results from their efforts when that candidate takes office. Sometimes, volunteerism can lead to activism. A young volunteer can become so involved in an issue that he or she soon begins marching in protest and leading demonstrations. But there is no level of involvement that is "right" or "wrong." Some young people are very satisfied to devote a few hours to an ongoing community project, while others become inspired to work long hours in order to fulfill what they believe is an unfulfilled need.

Why Volunteer?

Why spend Saturday participating in a walk-a-thon? Isn't spending time at the mall much more fun? Why help make quilts to raise money for AIDS research? Why not go to the movies instead? Why tutor a child who can't read? Isn't it more fun to try out the new skateboard park?

When young people enter their teen years, many of them begin to open their eyes to what is going on in the world around them. The experiences of most elementary school students are limited, and they are mainly concerned with their own wants and needs. As teens, though, many young people start noticing the differences between themselves and others. Independent Sector reported: "Teens had a higher volunteer rate than average (at least 70% compared with 59%) if they believed that social problems like poverty and hopelessness can be overcome through volunteer efforts; felt a moral duty to help people who suffer; or believed that it is within their power to do things that improve the welfare of others."

Young people often harbor personal reasons for volunteering. Many teens told the Independent Sector researchers that they volunteered because someone in their family became ill or needed help in some other way, or that they personally needed help and a volunteer came to their assistance. "The reasons teens cited most frequently for volunteering were: feeling compassion towards people in need; doing something for a cause that was important to them; and believing that if they helped others, others would help

Media coverage of the September 11, 2001, terrorist attacks helped spark an upswing in teenage volunteerism. At Ground Zero—the site where the World Trade Center had stood in New York—teenagers and adults worked side by side to help prepare food for rescue workers.

them," the Independent Sector report said. "Two out of three respondents cited the following major reasons for being kind and caring: 'Society is better off when we care for each other,' and 'It makes me feel good about myself when I care for others.'"

The September 11, 2001, terrorist attacks on the World Trade Center and Pentagon are believed to have been responsible for an upswing in teen volunteerism. For weeks, news coverage of the tragedy showed the activities of thousands of volunteers who streamed into New York and Washington, D.C., to assist in the rescue efforts. In the two months following the terrorist attacks, applications for AmeriCorps positions increased by 30 percent. Studies have found that other traumatic events worldwide, such as famine in Africa or conflict in the Middle East, can influence teens to become involved.

In August 2003, the Gallup Youth Survey asked 517 young people between the ages of 13 and 17 to share their thoughts about the qualities necessary to keep America strong. A total of 22 percent of the respondents said widespread volunteerism was "extremely important" in keeping America strong. Another 23 percent of the respondents said it was "extremely important" for citizens to serve in the military—which is, after all, another form of volunteerism.

Rewards for Volunteers

The rewards for volunteering cannot be measured in the short term. According to the Independent Sector report, the experience and knowledge gained from volunteering become an integral part of a young person's character. "As a result of their volunteer efforts, teens reported doing better in school or improving grades, developing new career goals, and learning about career options," the report said. "Other significant benefits included: learning how to respect others; learning to be helpful and kind; understanding people who are different from themselves; finding opportunities to develop leadership skills; becoming more patient; and understanding the qualities of good citizenship."

There are tangible rewards as well. For example, the college admissions process is one area where community service counts. Certainly, test scores and grades continue to be the most important factors that will determine whether a student is accepted into college, but a résumé that includes community service experience is likely to impress most college admissions officials. Most teenagers recognize this: a 2002 report by the Higher Education Research Institute of the University of California at Los Angeles found that 83 percent of college freshman reported performing volunteer work in their senior year of high school. "If you're looking at two middling kids whose grades aren't so great and one has tremendous community service and the other doesn't, you'll take the kid with the community service," explains Chris Hooker-Haring, the dean of admissions at Muhlenberg College. "One, because you'll have to assume they've learned something that will be valuable on the campus, and two, they'll have some inclinations and energies that will add something to the campus."

New Talents

Many times, teens discover new talents through volunteer work. Young people learn how to use tools when they help build a playground. Teenagers may learn they have a gift for instruction when they serve as volunteer tutors, or discover they have management skills that will be useful as they grow older and join the working world. A teenager's first job as a volunteer may be the first time he or she is expected to act responsibly.

Through volunteering, teenagers may discover new interests. The experiences of these volunteers with the Florida Keys Marine Mammal Rescue Team, shown rescuing a stranded pygmy whale, may inspire one of them to pursue a career in marine biology or a related field.

Many teens also learn a lot about themselves. Sixteen-year-old Adam Weber admitted to a reporter for *Education Week* magazine that he did not know what to make of homeless people until he started serving dinner to them at a program sponsored by the Youth Services Opportunities Project (YSOP) of New York. He had not been exposed to homelessness in his suburban California hometown, where he attends a private school. "It's scary at first when you're watching them come in," Weber said. "It takes a small amount of courage to even initiate contact. Once you get over that, these are just regular guys despite their financial situation. I don't try to feel sorry for them. I try to just treat them like buddies — that's the way I'd like to be treated."

Programs like YSOP are "not just about giving a couple of hours and walking away," explains Muzzy Rosenblatt, acting commissioner for the New York City Department of Homeless Shelters. "It helps young people be challenged well beyond the weekend. They ask: 'What is my government doing, what should government be doing? What are different faith-based organizations doing?' "

Another teenager who learned a lot about the problems of others through her volunteer work was Jennifer Brophy, a student at Ball State University in Indiana. She volunteered to tutor ninth-grade remedial science students at a high school in Frederick, Maryland. She kept a diary, which was eventually published in *Dig*, an Iowa-based newsletter. Early in her experience, Jennifer wrote that she felt frustrated. "Overall, tutoring is not what I expected," she said. "I thought the students would look up to me because I was older and could help them get through this course with a passing grade. This could not have been further from the truth. They are disrespectful, loud, annoying, and I detest being near them."

Slowly, though, the students warmed up to Jennifer, and she began to appreciate their problems. She wrote that some students showed progress while others did not seem to care about their studies. Soon, Jennifer realized she could not work miracles with the students, and she came to cherish the little victories. "David decided to cooperate with me, and we got further than anybody else," Jennifer wrote at the end of the class. "He's bossy — and I shouldn't put up with him telling me what to do. But he probably needs somebody to listen to him. I'm certain he will do well on the final if he applies himself, and decides to care. I would like to learn more about motivating students to want to succeed and stay in school. I want to be able to serve the students next year so much better."

Chapter Two

This Illinois hospital is filled with volunteers waiting to give blood to help the victims of the September 11, 2001, terrorist attacks. Americans have had a long tradition of community service.

A Tradition of Volunteerism

One of the volunteers who flocked to New York City in the aftermath of the September 11 terrorist attack was Ryan Morra, a recent high school graduate from Connecticut. He was assigned by the Family Assistance Center of New York to interview families of the victims, to help determine who was eligible for financial assistance. "It's been quite intense and emotionally exhausting," Ryan told a reporter for the *Christian Science Monitor*. "There's nothing better that I can be doing with my time right now than helping these people."

Ryan had joined the Family Assistance Center through AmeriCorps, a federal agency that provides volunteers to local and national nonprofit organizations in the United States. AmeriCorps volunteers, who can be as young as 17, must make a commitment to the agency to work a minimum of 10 months. In return, they are given a small living allowance, but at the conclusion of their commitment they can receive money for college tuition or expenses. As of 2012, the maximum education award provided by AmeriCorps was $5,550.

A History of Service

Young Americans made a commitment to public service long before federal agencies like AmeriCorps were established to recruit them. In fact, young people volunteered their services when the American colonies were still ruled by Great Britain. Boys often joined their fathers to fight in the American Revolution. One of them was James Monroe, an 18-year-old student at the College of William and Mary in Virginia, who dropped out to volunteer for the Continental Army in 1776. Before the end of the year Monroe had earned the rank of lieutenant and was wounded at the Battle of Trenton while leading a charge to capture enemy cannons. He would later become the fifth president of the United States. Over the next two centuries, many other young men would readily volunteer for military service.

In small towns and big cities throughout the United States, volunteers provided many of the first civil services. The first New York City policemen were volunteers. Most city and small-town firemen were volunteers; many still are today. Religious leaders instilled in their congregations a strong commitment to charity and helping the less fortunate, and churches provided volunteers for many purposes.

The early 1800s saw the establishment of community volunteer societies, many of which were organized to provide medical care to the poor. Other groups formed to fight slavery. Many of the first abolitionist societies provided volunteer lawyers to defend blacks charged with being fugitive slaves. When the Underground

Railroad was created to help runaway slaves escape to freedom in Canada, it was volunteers who made it work. Of course, when the Civil War broke out thousands of volunteers streamed into the ranks on both sides.

Following the Civil War, the growth of cities due to industrialization began to cause many social problems. Immigrants seeking a better life in the United States found homes in the cities, but the overcrowded and dirty areas in which they lived lacked basic services like clean water. In 1896, social reformers Ballington and Maud Booth established Volunteers of America to make sure people living in city tenement districts had enough to eat, a place to sleep, and proper health care. The group organized day nurseries for children, provided housing for single men and women, and established the first halfway houses for recently released prison inmates.

James Monroe dropped out of college to volunteer for the Continental Army during the American War for Independence. He would later be elected the fifth president of the United States.

In 1964 President Lyndon B. Johnson signed the Economic Opportunity Act. This legislation created Volunteers in Service to America (VISTA), which recruited volunteers to work in underdeveloped areas within the United States.

During World War II, many able-bodied men were drafted and sent overseas to fight, so people who remained at home volunteered to support the war effort. Housewives went to work in factories. Civilians patrolled streets at night, enforcing blackouts and curfews. Children went door-to-door selling bonds to raise money. Hollywood stars toured war zones to entertain the troops.

American Volunteers Go Abroad

During the 1960s, the U.S. government served notice that it intended to actively recruit volunteers for public service. In January 1961, President John F. Kennedy challenged Americans in his inaugural speech to "Ask not what your country can do for you—ask what you can do for your country." Two months later, he signed an executive order creating the Peace Corps. This agency's mandate was to recruit and train volunteers and send them to underdeveloped nations for humanitarian purposes.

Today, some 8,000 Peace Corps volunteers are working in more than 70 different countries. The volunteers, who make a two-year commitment to public service, can be as young as 18. They are sent into foreign lands where they work as teachers, carpenters, health care workers, farm supervisors, and similar roles.

If the Peace Corps could work in Guatemala and Ghana, why couldn't it work in Arkansas and Arizona? That was the question asked by President Lyndon B. Johnson, who succeeded Kennedy in 1963. Johnson proposed a domestic organization in which volunteers would work with poor people in rural and urban areas. In 1964, Johnson signed the Economic Opportunity Act, creating a number of anti-poverty programs. One of the programs created by the new law was Volunteers in Service to America, or VISTA.

On December 12, 1964, the president welcomed the first 20 VISTA volunteers in a reception at the White House. Johnson told them, "Your pay will be low; the conditions of your labor often will be difficult. But you will have the satisfaction of leading a great national effort and you will have the ultimate reward which comes to those who serve their fellow man." The youngest VISTA volunteer standing in the White House that day was 18; the oldest 81. After six weeks of training, they were sent to an urban neighborhood in Connecticut, rural communities in Kentucky, and a migrant farm labor camp in California. By the end of the first year of the program, 2,000 VISTA volunteers were on the job.

The Development of AmeriCorps

Johnson wasn't the only president to support volunteerism. An important part of Jimmy Carter's presidency was his commitment to human rights. After leaving the White House in 1981, Carter became an active participant in Habitat for Humanity International, an organization that builds houses for low-income families. In 1984, the former president picked up a hammer and helped renovate a six-story building in New York City, providing shelter for 19 families. He has since become the organization's most prominent ambassador.

JOINING AMERICORPS

Most AmeriCorps programs are open to anyone 17 and older. Young people who are accepted into the program can select from a list of 1,000 organizations that need AmeriCorps volunteers. Administrators try to match applicants with their areas of interest. Typical organizations that employ AmeriCorps volunteers are the American Red Cross, Habitat for Humanity, and Boys and Girls Clubs.

Most AmeriCorps volunteers serve commitments of 10 months to a year, although some participants stay longer. Also, some participants are able to work out part-time arrangements with the agencies that employ them. For the most part, though, AmeriCorps volunteers are expected to provide full-time attention for the lengths of their commitments. Payment during the term of commitment is minimal: volunteers are given a subsidy that helps pay their living expenses. Some of the programs provide housing.

AmeriCorps members who enroll in the National Service Trust are eligible to receive an education award upon completion of their commitments. The education award can be used to pay college tuition and expenses or repay student loans. As of 2012, the award was

As a college student at Georgetown University during the 1960s, Bill Clinton volunteered to drive food and medical supplies into riot-torn neighborhoods of Washington, D.C. A year after Clinton was elected president, he encouraged Congress to pass the National and Community Service Trust Act of 1993. The legislation established a new agency, the Corporation for National and Community Service, which absorbed VISTA and other federally based volunteer programs. VISTA was renamed AmeriCorps. As an incentive, volunteers were provided a modest living allowance of about $9,300 a year and promised financial aid for college if they successfully completed their commitments to the program.

AmeriCorps volunteers fanned out across the United States, laboring on such projects as cutting trails through state parks,

$5,550 for a year of full-time service, with lesser awards for part-time and reduced part-time service. A member has up to seven years after his or her term of service has ended to claim the award. Some AmeriCorps members who elect not to take the education award are eligible for a cash award of $100 for each month they served in the program, up to $1,200.

Only U.S. citizens or legal permanent residents are eligible to join AmeriCorps. Some programs may require special skills, but for the most part AmeriCorps agencies are simply looking for people willing to work hard. AmeriCorps provides some training to participants; most of the agencies that employ the volunteers will train them as well.

Young people can submit an application to AmeriCorps online by going to the organization's World Wide Web page at http://www.americorps.gov. AmeriCorps can also be contacted through the headquarters of the Corporation for National and Community Service, 1201 New York Avenue NW, Washington, DC, 20525. The phone number is 202-606-5000.

building playgrounds, mentoring inner-city children, painting schools, and doing emergency services work such as flood control. By 2013, the 20-year anniversary of the program, more than 800,000 AmeriCorps members had been recruited, trained, and put to work. Eventually, Clinton would say that of all his accomplishments as president, he was most proud of creating AmeriCorps: "I had a dream that I could give young people in this country a chance to serve in their communities, to help children, to make places safer, to make the schools work better, to deal with the health problems and the worries and the fears of our children and build up their hopes, and at the same time earn a little money for a college education. And that's how AmeriCorps was born."

There have been bumps along the way. AmeriCorps supporters had to endure the skepticism of some members of Congress, who questioned whether the federal government should be paying people to volunteer. "To me, a volunteer at a church or something, they get coffee and doughnuts," said California congressman Randy Cunningham. "When you define 'volunteer,' let's make sure volunteer is volunteer—not paid." That type of attitude often resulted in budget cuts for AmeriCorps programs. In 2002, hundreds of AmeriCorps programs were slashed after administrators found they had the money for only 30,000 volunteer positions. (They had expected to fund 75,000 positions.) In 2003, Congress increased funding for AmeriCorps by about 50 percent, providing the agency with a budget of $444 million. By 2012, the annual operating budget for AmeriCorps stood at about $470 million. However, Republicans in Congress called for eliminating the program entirely.

For their part, young people have been supportive of a national community service plan, according to results of Gallup polls. In

2000, 51 percent of teens who responded to a Gallup Youth Survey said they favored a national community or military service requirement for all young people for a full year.

Setting an Example

At the age of 17, Ricky Recchia, a New York City AmeriCorps volunteer, worked as a group leader for the After School Corporation. He was given the job of tutoring children at two New York schools. "AmeriCorps gave me the opportunity to volunteer in my own neighborhood and give back," Recchia told a reporter for *Newsweek* magazine. "And that's a big thing."

Dianna Ball took a year off from graduate school to work for an AmeriCorps project in Baltimore, Maryland. "During training we

Utilizing volunteer workers and donated materials, Habitat for Humanity builds homes for low-income families all over the United States. These volunteers in Snoqualmie, Washington, are being briefed before beginning work for the day.

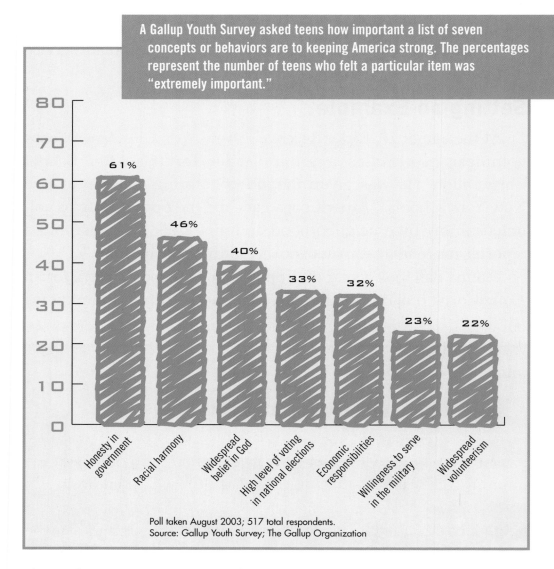

A Gallup Youth Survey asked teens how important a list of seven concepts or behaviors are to keeping America strong. The percentages represent the number of teens who felt a particular item was "extremely important."

61% Honesty in government
46% Racial harmony
40% Widespread belief in God
33% High level of voting in national elections
32% Economic responsibilities
23% Willingness to serve in the military
22% Widespread volunteerism

Poll taken August 2003; 517 total respondents.
Source: Gallup Youth Survey; The Gallup Organization

cleaned up an inner city neighborhood," said Ball. "I grew up across the street from a cow farm. I had never really experienced life in the inner city before and I was a little nervous. . . . About two hours into our work, a man came out of one of the houses and asked what we were doing. We explained and he asked if he could help. His offer changed the way I felt about what I was doing. I went about my work with a new purpose. Not only was I cleaning the neighborhood, I was setting an example and introducing the possibility of lasting impact by involving the community members."

And Karen McCall, a student majoring in social work at Delaware State University, said she realized that AmeriCorps could provide her with valuable on-the-job training. She joined the AmeriCorps Crossroads program on her university campus. "AmeriCorps Crossroads is a . . . community based program that does everything from mentoring, to fixing up homes, to providing senior services for the community," McCall explained. "We also participate in Adopt-a-Highway, Earth Day, and other days of service. I am a team leader and oversee 13 members. Managing my time is a constant challenge, but it is well worth the joy I get out of the work. I love working with seniors. We talk, sometimes I read the Bible to them. I enjoy listening to their stories and getting to know them as people."

New Opportunities to Volunteer

In 1997, President Clinton decided to take the nation's commitment to volunteerism a step further when he convened the Summit for America's Future in Philadelphia. The summit was held to explore new ways Americans could dedicate themselves to helping less-fortunate people. The outcome of the summit was the establishment of America's Promise, an organization founded by Clinton and former presidents Carter, George H. W. Bush, and Gerald Ford. It was headed by Colin Powell, who would later become secretary of state.

America's Promise dedicates its resources to helping children. Powell has used his influence to convince many of the largest U.S. corporations to make financial commitments to programs that fit

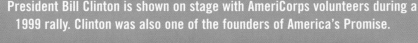

President Bill Clinton is shown on stage with AmeriCorps volunteers during a 1999 rally. Clinton was also one of the founders of America's Promise.

into its criteria. To qualify for America's Promise support, a non-profit group must develop ongoing relationships between young people and adults; provide safe places with structured activities during non-school hours; ensure that participants receive adequate nutrition, exercise, and health care; work with youths to improve skills they can use to further their education or find employment; and boost the confidence and self-esteem of the participants so that they will have a heightened sense of responsibility.

Among the corporations and groups that made pledges were the cable music channel VH1, which said it would provide $1 million to a New York City music education program; Taco Bell, which opened six centers to provide teenagers with after-school activities and job training programs; the National Football League Players Association, which said it would establish a mentoring program connecting professional athletes with Native American teenagers; and eyeglasses retailer LensCrafters, which said it would provide a million people, mostly children, with free vision care.

When George W. Bush took office as president in January 2001, he also proved to be committed to volunteerism. Shortly after he graduated from college, Bush spent several months working for the Professional United Leadership League (PULL), a Houston-based group that recruited professional athletes to work with inner-city young people. PULL also maintained a clubhouse in Houston and provided a number of day programs for students, such as tutoring and motivational classes.

As president, Bush established the USA Freedom Corps with a mission to match potential volunteers with organizations that need their help. In his 2002 State of the Union Address, and during the months that followed, Bush challenged all Americans to provide 4,000 hours of community service during their lifetimes. "We want to be a nation that serves goals larger than self," Bush declared.

In April 2009, President Bush's successor, Barack Obama, signed into law the Edward M. Kennedy Serve America Act. Among other provisions, it expanded AmeriCorps and significantly increased funding for the Corporation for National and Community Service. "All that's required on your part," Obama said to would-be volunteers, "is a willingness to make a difference. That is, after all, the beauty of service. Anyone can do it."

Chapter Three

Amherst College freshmen work on a Massachusetts farm as part of their school's community service project. As more schools make community service mandatory, some people question the practice of forcing young people to volunteer.

When Volunteering Is Mandatory

As a senior at Rye High School in New York, Nick Loddo logged some 1,100 hours of community service, volunteering mostly in an ambulance corps but also spending his free time cleaning beaches. "Once you start, it's hard to stop," Loddo told a newspaper reporter in 1990. "I make time to volunteer."

Another Rye senior, Bana Mouwakey, spent 450 hours working in a food pantry and a homeless shelter. Mouwakey was so dedicated that she became president of a club known as SUSTAIN—Students Undertaking Services To Aid Those In Need.

At the same time, Rye student Dana Murphy spent her senior year working with preschool children at a church day-care center. Murphy told a reporter that she had been thinking about becoming an educator and used this experience to see whether she would enjoy the teaching profession. "I love it," she said. "I didn't want to spend four years in college and then find out I didn't like it."

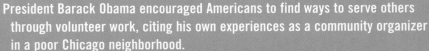

President Barack Obama encouraged Americans to find ways to serve others through volunteer work, citing his own experiences as a community organizer in a poor Chicago neighborhood.

However, many other Rye students "volunteered" with far less enthusiasm, because at Rye High School community service is mandatory. To graduate, students must perform 60 hours of community service between the ninth and twelfth grades. It is as much a part of their curriculum as mathematics, science, and social studies. "It's an extra, unnecessary burden students don't need," grumbled Rye senior John C. Anderson. Other students agreed, arguing that after-school jobs and other commitments leave them no time to devote to volunteerism. "It's a pain," said senior Kim Sweenie. "When you are forced into this, it doesn't make sense."

Across the country, many high schools and colleges have made community service part of their graduation requirement. In

Maryland, state officials mandated it for all high school students. In most cases, the community service requirement has been met with howls of protest from students and parents. Conservative columnists and lawmakers have denounced mandatory community service as a violation of civil rights, likening it to indentured servitude and even slavery. "It reminds me of something they used to do in the Soviet Union," Barrie Ciliberti, a conservative Maryland lawmaker, told *Time* magazine in 1997. "Every Saturday, you will volunteer to help the greater glory of the state."

Although lawsuits have been filed, judges have consistently upheld the right of a school district to require students to perform community service. As a result, it is believed that more than a million students a year take part in school-mandated community service projects.

Becoming Socially Engaged

School districts started requiring community service by students following a 1987 report by the Carnegie Foundation for the Advancement of Teaching, which recommended that all high school students be required to perform 120 hours of volunteer work. "We were struck during our study that teenagers can go through 12 years of formal education without becoming socially engaged, without spending time with older people who may be lonely, helping a child who has not learned to read, cleaning up the litter on the street, or even rendering some useful service to the school itself," wrote Ernest Boyer, president of the foundation. "This life of detachment occurs at the very time students are deciding who they are and where they fit in."

How did high school students become so insensitive to less-fortunate people? Lynda McDonnell, a journalist and lecturer in social issues at the University of Minnesota, blamed prosperity. McDonnell found that most of her students were out of touch with poverty because they had never experienced it. She found that only a small number of students in her class could truly say they were born into impoverished circumstances. Many of McDonnell's students had never encountered a poor person on the street, been approached by a homeless man looking for a handout, or seen for themselves the hopeless circumstances of America's poorest people.

"Their grandparents might have been children during the Depression, but they didn't talk about it," McDonnell wrote in an essay published in 2000 in *Washington Monthly* magazine. "Perhaps, like my sons' grandparents, they live far away and want to spend their limited family time spoiling their grandchildren with miniature golf and ice cream, not recounting hard times. High school history does a poor job of filling in the gaps."

In the essay, McDonnell cited a 1998 study by the University of California at Los Angeles in which researchers found that just 17 percent of freshmen at the school reported an interest in "influencing the political structure" while less than a third of the respondents believed that "promoting racial understanding" was an important goal in life. What did young college students want most to accomplish in life? The most popular response in the UCLA study was to be "well off financially."

According to McDonnell, a large share of the blame for this lack of teenager interest in improving society lay with adults. "Our children learn their values from us, after all, and those of us who marched on Washington . . . haven't carried the habit of activism into adulthood," she wrote. "Our kids are more likely to see us staying late at the office, working out at the gym, or rushing through dinner and hauling them to soccer practice than signing up for political committee assignments."

Many school officials were influenced by the Carnegie Foundation report. In Rye, for example, then-principal Deane Flood had spent two years in the 1960s as a Peace Corps volunteer in Brazil. Flood took the Carnegie report to the Rye School Board and convinced members to authorize a 60-hour community service requirement for the high school.

As a result of the Carnegie Foundation report, students across the United States found themselves performing community service.

Many U.S. teenagers are not familiar with the hardships of poverty because they have never experienced them firsthand. Some young people are shocked to learn that, as of 2012, there were about 640,000 homeless people living in the United States.

In Maryland, which requires 75 hours of service for graduation, junior Dale Davis found herself working in a Calvert County homeless shelter. Her duties required her to sort through piles of old clothes that were donated to the shelter and throwaway items that were just too worn out even to give to a homeless person. "Yeah, these clothes can really start to stink after awhile," Dale told *Scholastic Update* magazine. "But I figure somebody's got to do this. So why not me?"

Is it Fair to Require Community Service?

Not everybody agrees with the Carnegie Foundation report and the response of schools. Paul Saunders founded Citizens Against Mandatory Service (CAMS) in 1990 when the Bethlehem Area School District in Pennsylvania mandated a community service requirement of 60 hours for each high school student. Saunders' group sued the school district, alleging that mandatory volunteerism violates the Thirteenth Amendment to the U.S. Constitution, which outlawed slavery and involuntary servitude. When two federal judges refused to overturn the school district's policy, CAMS asked the U.S. Supreme Court to hear its argument, but the nation's highest court refused to consider the matter.

"The wide acceptance of mandatory servitude in today's culture is the result of the marriage of two intellectual movements: Marxism and religion," Saunders said in a 1998 interview with *Capitalism Magazine*. "Both groups accept the tenet that moral worth arises out of fulfilling your duty to live for others, which ultimately results in living for the state, the government. . . . All that is possible in today's culture is awakening the public to the fact that mandatory servitude violates the rational American values of self-reliance, self-sufficiency, self-confidence, self-motivation — in a word, selfishness."

The Ayn Rand Institute, based in Irvine, California, has lobbied for years against compulsory community service. Rand was the author of such novels as *The Fountainhead* and *Atlas Shrugged*, which are staples of many high school literature classes. The institute was founded by supporters of Rand's philosophy of "Objectivism," which places the rights of individuals over those of the state. In an essay written for the institute, Baltimore attorney Thomas A. Bowden wrote, "Proponents of forced service insist that it is really for the students' own good. For example, the Bethlehem program claimed that compulsory service helps students 'develop pride in assisting others.' But does anyone really believe that students will develop pride by succumbing to orders, abandoning their own personal projects, and serving the needs of strangers? The true source of pride is the achievement of one's own values."

Although the opponents of mandatory community service lost the Bethlehem case, hard feelings remained in the school district for years. In 1997, two seniors were denied diplomas in the school district because they refused to meet the community service requirement. It is likely that one of the students, Kathie Moralis, would have been named valedictorian had she met her high school's community service requirement. She earned a 4.81 grade point average (GPA) by carrying straight As and taking advanced placement courses, which are given weighted credit when determining GPA.

Ironically, Moralis did perform volunteer work while in high school, but she refused to register her volunteer time with the school's community service program, believing the requirement was morally wrong. Moralis was granted a general equivalency diploma and received a scholarship to study chemistry at Penn State. As for her stance on the Bethlehem community service requirement, Moralis told a reporter in 1997, "I don't regret it. I couldn't face myself for the next 10 years if I gave in."

Criticism of Mandatory Service

Mandatory community service faces other criticisms than philosophical arguments about the rights of the individual. People who run social service agencies — the groups that are supposed to benefit from the student volunteers — sometimes question whether their young helpers are truly getting the message. "Anyone who wants to get out there and lend a helping hand, please do," Jessica Gavora, director of programs for the conservative study group New Citizens Project, told *Scholastic Update* magazine in 1997. "But do it out of concern for your fellow man. Don't do it because the government wants you to." And Scott Bullock, a Washington, D.C., lawyer, wondered in the same article whether school administrators weren't being unfair to poor students. "Forcing people to do good works is a sure way to destroy the spirit of volunteering," he said. "If parents want their kids to work for charities after school, then let them. But what about the low-income kids who work after school? It's not the role of public schools to say what's good for one kid is good for every kid."

Also, some critics have complained that the schools don't do a very good job of administering the programs—that the definition

Two high school students and a teacher stand waist-deep in a creek, catching organisms for a science class. In some school programs, students can earn credit toward their mandatory community service by doing extra-curricular work for their classes.

of community service often becomes vague because school administrators are willing to accept almost any form of volunteering from students scrambling to meet their requirements. For example, some schools permit students to count the time they spend in school activities toward their community service requirement. This might mean that a clarinet player in the school band gets to count rehearsal time toward his requirement. Indeed, the school may also permit the clarinet player to count the time he spends playing music in the grandstand during football games. It often goes further than that. Students in biology classes may get credit if the teacher decides, on a spring day, to lead everyone outside where they spend their class time planting flowers along a public sidewalk. Some students even get credit for the time they spend in math club or the debate society.

And still another criticism of mandatory community service centers on the value of the work provided by students. Consider the case of Christina Mullins, who was interviewed by *Time* magazine in 1997. Mullins, a student at Dunbar High School in Baltimore, was considering a career in medicine so she volunteered to work in the obstetrics-gynecology department at Johns Hopkins University. But all Mullins found herself doing was working in the file room. "I was filing papers all day—eight hours—for free," Mullins told *Time*. "Do you know how boring that is? And I couldn't get a job because I had to get my hours. I had no money in 1996."

Despite the criticisms, many students would appear to have accepted mandatory community service. A Gallup Youth Survey conducted in 2000 found that 48 percent of the respondents performed some type of community service. That included 16 percent who did volunteer work through a school-sponsored program, 19 percent who worked outside the school programs, and 13 percent who volunteered in both situations.

Overall, 31 percent of the respondents—29 percent of boys and 34 percent of girls—said they were required by their schools to perform community service. The Gallup Organization found girls much more enthusiastic about volunteering. Overall, 33 percent of the respondents said they volunteered for social service activities

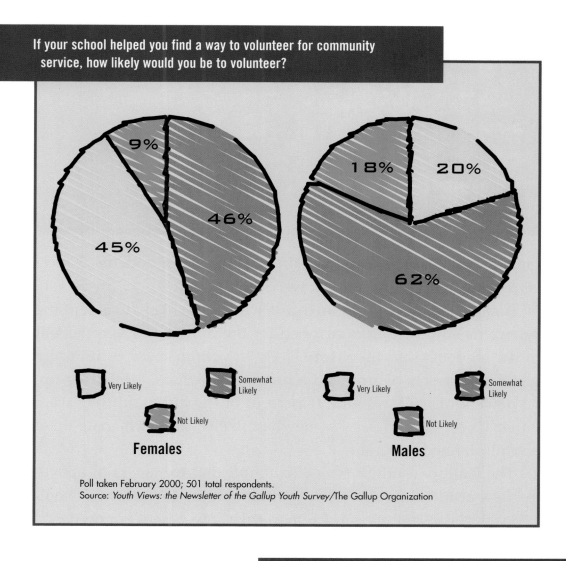

If your school helped you find a way to volunteer for community service, how likely would you be to volunteer?

9%

46%

45%

18% 20%

62%

☐ Very Likely   ▨ Somewhat Likely   ▨ Not Likely

Females

☐ Very Likely   ▨ Somewhat Likely   ▨ Not Likely

Males

Poll taken February 2000; 501 total respondents.
Source: *Youth Views: the Newsletter of the Gallup Youth Survey*/The Gallup Organization

A student helps to organize donated canned food during a food drive. In many high schools, community service has become a requirement for graduation.

outside of what their school required. Of those respondents, 30 percent were boys and 35 percent were girls.

As for the school programs, girls were more likely to accept the programs administrators planned for them. Eighty-seven percent of the students said they were likely to volunteer for community service if the school arranged a program for them. Of that group, 82 percent of the boys and 91 percent of the girls said they were either "very likely" or "somewhat likely" to participate in a school-planned program.

The Gallup Youth Survey also found that teenagers of above-average academic standing were more willing to perform school-sponsored community service than their lower-performing peers.

A total of 34 percent of the high achievers said they would perform school-sponsored community service while 27 percent of the lower-achieving students said they were willing to volunteer in school-sponsored programs. In addition, 38 percent of the high achievers said they would volunteer outside the school program, while just 24 percent of the lower-performing students said they would be willing to give up their free time for community service projects. The results of the 2000 survey were based on interviews with 500 young people between the ages of 13 and 17.

Community Service in College

If students believe they will leave community service behind once they finish high school, they may be mistaken. More and more colleges are emphasizing community service, and many are making it a requirement for graduation. For example, Elmira College in New York requires all freshmen to perform 60 hours of community service. Wittenberg University in Ohio insists that all students perform 27 hours of volunteer work over the course of a single semester. At the University of Connecticut School of Medicine, all students are required to perform 15 hours of community service in a health-related field.

The University of California at Santa Barbara requires students enrolled in the honors program to perform 20 to 40 hours of community service during their junior and senior years. Fraternity members at UC Santa Barbara are expected to perform 32 hours of community service a year. In addition, each fraternity is required to donate 35 percent of its budget to charity.

All students at the College of the Atlantic in Maine must complete 40 hours of volunteer work before their last term of enrollment. The school's course catalog explains, "The College feels

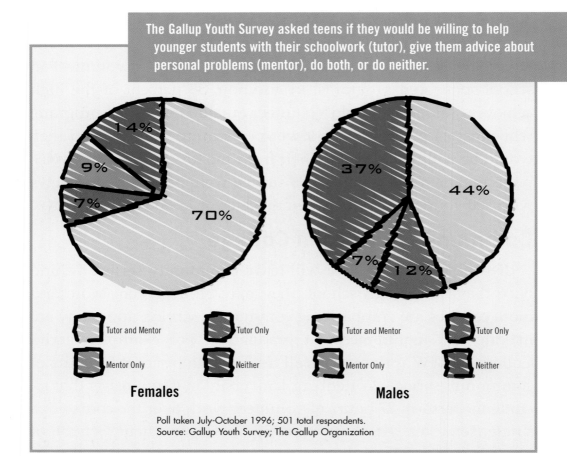

The Gallup Youth Survey asked teens if they would be willing to help younger students with their schoolwork (tutor), give them advice about personal problems (mentor), do both, or do neither.

14%

9%

7%

70%

37%

44%

7%

12%

Tutor and Mentor

Tutor Only

Mentor Only

Neither

Tutor and Mentor

Tutor Only

Mentor Only

Neither

Females

Males

Poll taken July–October 1996; 501 total respondents.
Source: Gallup Youth Survey; The Gallup Organization

strongly that community service provides valuable experience as well as personal and educational opportunities that complement a student's studies in the field of Human Ecology."

Just as many high school students welcome the opportunity to perform community service—whether their school requires it or not—many college students also look forward to volunteering as often as they can. For example, 130 volunteers from 10 colleges in the Orlando, Florida, area regularly pitch in at Anthony House, a homeless shelter where students have repaired a playground and cooked meals for the residents. Recently, 120 students from

DePaul University in Chicago signed up to work in homeless shelters and retirement communities from Canada to Kentucky. Thirteen female students from Mount Holyoke College in Massachusetts traveled to Birmingham, Alabama, where they rebuilt a church that had burned to the ground. More than 100 students from the University of Vermont signed up to deliver food to AIDS patients in Washington, D.C., and run violence prevention workshops for teenagers in Detroit. And during spring break, many young people give up their time to help others. A student at Boston College explained to a reporter from *U.S. News and World Report* why each year she spent her break helping to build homes in rural Appalachian communities: "It's amazing to come from a rich school and find an area of the United States where they have no running water."

Chapter Four

Armed forces recruiters search public places and schools for potential recruits. In this photo at a mall in Miami, a recruiter for the U.S. Marines speaks with a young woman about enlisting.

The Call to Arms: Teens and the Military

When Jim Beverly was a high school senior in Akron, Ohio, he told his mother and father that he intended to join the U.S. Army soon after graduation. Jim's father, Charles Beverly, was a veteran of the Vietnam War. He felt the army would be a good experience for his son, mostly because of the educational opportunities the service promised. Jim's mother, Jocelyn Perge, was far less enthusiastic. She knew being a soldier was a risky occupation, made even more so because of the "war on terrorism" and U.S. military involvement in Afghanistan. Nonetheless, she told a reporter from *Time* magazine, "I'm proud of him for doing what he believed in."

Beverly enlisted in the summer of 2002, two days after he turned 18. By late 2003, he had been promoted to private first class and was assigned to a platoon patrolling Baghdad, Iraq, searching for insurgents who continued to wage war after the collapse of Saddam Hussein's regime. On the night of December 10, 2003, 19-year-old Beverly was in a three-vehicle convoy making its way through the streets of Baghdad. Part of their mission was to draw fire and make the insurgents give away their positions.

For about an hour, the mission was uneventful. The soldiers in the platoon saw no signs of insurgents. But then, after the convoy became stuck in traffic in the crowded al-Adhamiya neighborhood, someone tossed a grenade into the open bed of the Humvee in which Beverly was riding. Shrapnel ricocheted through the vehicle, wounding Beverly and three others. A medic in the trailing Humvee rushed forward to administer first aid, and the convoy soon sped away to safety.

Hours later in Ohio, Charles Beverly received a phone call from his son. Jim had been hit in the right hand and right knee by shrapnel, and the explosion had knocked out two of his teeth. As Jim told his father about the grenade attack, and the fact that the army had decided to award him a medal for his battle wounds, Charles Beverly was just grateful that his son was alive.

A Long History of Service

Young Americans have been volunteering to defend their country since the Minutemen answered the call to arms at Lexington and Concord during the American Revolution. It has only been relatively recently, though, that the United States military has relied entirely on volunteers. Over the course of U.S. history, most of the nation's wars have been fought by armed forces composed largely of draftees—young men who were required by law to serve in the military. That changed shortly after American involvement in the Vietnam War ended in 1973. Congress abolished the draft, although all men between the ages of 18 and 25 still have to register with the U.S. Selective Service System, the agency that would administer the draft should Congress reauthorize compulsory military service.

A few politicians did, in fact, call for a resumption of the draft in the years after 2003. The United States was involved in grinding conflicts in two countries, Iraq and Afghanistan, and a relatively small number of soldiers and marines bore the brunt of the fighting. As the wars dragged on, these soldiers and marines faced repeated combat deployments, which—even if the service members were fortunate enough to avoid death or serious injury—often took a toll on their mental health, family life, and morale. Critics said it wasn't fair that a very small proportion of the nation's people were being asked to take all the risks and make all

For most of U.S. history, the military has drafted young people to serve. However, during the Vietnam War many young Americans refused to take part in the draft because they felt the war was immoral. This photo was taken at a protest in 1965. The draft ended in 1973.

A young man speaks with a U.S. Army recruiter. For some young people, there is no higher aspiration than to serve the nation through a career in the military. For others, however, the decision to enlist is driven by factors such as the state of the U.S. job market.

the sacrifices in the country's wars, even if those people had volunteered to serve. A draft, the critics said, was needed.

Yet policymakers never seriously considered reinstituting the draft. And it is highly unlikely that compulsory military service will be brought back soon—if ever. For one thing, most top military leaders don't think the draft makes sense anymore. The U.S. military increasingly relies on high-tech equipment and systems. Even infantry soldiers now need an extensive set of skills to be effective. U.S. military leaders have said that it wouldn't be cost-effective to train recruits who'd likely leave the service after a year (the length of time Vietnam-era draftees were required to serve).

One reason young people volunteer for the armed services is from a sense of patriotism and desire to defend freedom. However, there are other reasons. The state of the U.S. economy, for example, is usually a more significant factor driving enlistment. When jobs are hard to come by, the prospect of a guaranteed paycheck in the armed services, along with the military's promise of future assistance with educational expenses, is often too good a deal for many teens to ignore.

"Students still see the military as a way to see the world and get an education or a certain skill," explained high school guidance counselor Libby Coffin.

Trends in Enlistment

When the economy is booming, military recruiters often have difficulty filling their quotas. To be sure, there are always people who find the idea of military service appealing. But joining the army, navy, air force, or marines is not the first choice of most young people. In a strong economy, when job opportunities are abundant, it's hard to entice these people to enlist.

The armed forces had trouble filling their ranks with qualified recruits during the last half of the 1990s, a period of economic growth and low unemployment. In 1999, for example, the army fell short of its recruitment target by about 6,300; the navy, by about 7,000.

In addition to the strong economy, some analysts attributed the recruitment shortfalls to cultural trends. Young people, they said, were in general more sedentary and less physically fit than previous generations had been. Hence they were more likely to be intimidated by the physical rigors of basic training, which all new recruits must undergo. Moreover, as many military officers observed, young people were not as accustomed to following authority; they were more resistant to regimentation. "It's the unwillingness to live an organized lifestyle. That's what gets them," lamented Major General John Van Alstyne, commander of Fort Jackson in South Carolina, a major Army training center.

The concept of the all-volunteer military may also have contributed to the decline in enlistment in the late 1990s. While the draft was in place, it was likely that a teenager's father was a veteran, drafted to serve in World War II, Korea, or Vietnam. Fathers are an important role model, and many young people were willing to join the military simply because their dad had served. The all-volunteer military, and corresponding reduction in the numbers of American troops, decreased the number of veterans heading typical American households.

But then came September 11. In January and February of 2003, as the United States and its allies were mobilizing to invade Iraq, the Gallup Youth Survey asked 1,200 young people between the ages of 13 and 17 their thoughts on volunteering for the military. Eleven percent of the respondents said they had a "great deal" of interest in serving in the military while 27 percent of the teens said they had "some" interest, for a total of 38 percent of young Americans favoring military service to some degree.

A few months later, the Gallup Youth Survey again visited the question of military service. In August 2003, 517 young people were asked about keeping America strong. By then, Iraqi dictator Saddam Hussein had been deposed; nevertheless, daily news reports carried stories about violence in Iraq against members of the American military. Still, 23 percent of the respondents said a "willingness to serve in the military" was necessary to keep America strong. It was hardly the top answer—responses such as honesty in government, racial harmony, and a belief in God all scored higher percentages. Yet in the survey young people expressed a degree of patriotism, and many said they were willing to commit their lives to keep the United States free and strong.

Attractiveness of Military Service

Along with the opportunity to serve their country, young Americans could earn tangible benefits by enlisting in the armed forces. For example, in addition to whatever job training they might receive while in uniform, service members could qualify for money to pay for up to 36 months of college under a law known as the Montgomery G.I. Bill. This benefit wouldn't necessarily cover the entire cost of obtaining a college degree. However, the U.S. Army, Navy,

Many young Americans enlist in the armed forces as a way to obtain financial aid for college. Slow economic conditions and a lack of jobs make military service an attractive option for many young people.

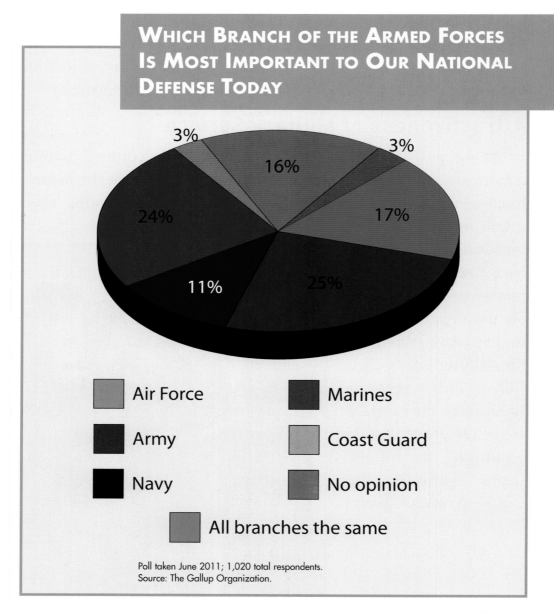

WHICH BRANCH OF THE ARMED FORCES IS MOST IMPORTANT TO OUR NATIONAL DEFENSE TODAY

3%

3%

16%

17%

24%

11%

25%

Air Force

Marines

Army

Coast Guard

Navy

No opinion

All branches the same

Poll taken June 2011; 1,020 total respondents.
Source: The Gallup Organization.

Marine Corps, and Coast Guard all have separate college funds, which eligible service members can tap to pay for college tuition and expenses. (The U.S. Air Force is alone among the five branches of the armed services in not having a separate college fund.)

The wave of patriotism that swept the country after the September 11 terrorist attacks, combined with relatively high unemployment in the years 2002–05, helped military recruiters easily fill their quotas. As is typically the case, the new recruits who entered the service during this period were mostly in their late teens or early twenties. Indeed, Americans age 17–19 formed a significant percentage of the armed services overall. In 2004, for example, about 12 percent of all personnel in the army, 10 percent of all personnel in the air force, and 12 percent of all personnel in the navy were 17 to 19 years old. For the Marine Corps, meanwhile, the figure approached 20 percent.

But the number of young people who wanted to join the military leveled off as the war in Iraq grew increasingly bloody — and increasingly unpopular in the United States. By 2006, the army had to lower its enlistment standards to meet recruitment targets. Volunteers who previously would have been rejected because they lacked a high school diploma, scored low on the army's aptitude test, had certain medical conditions, or even had a criminal record were now being accepted.

In 2008–09, however, the U.S. economy cratered, causing unemployment to spike. Enlistment standards were again raised as more young people looked to the military for a job.

By 2013, the U.S. Department of Defense was planning for a significantly smaller military. The army, for example, was projected to shrink from 562,000 to 490,000 people by 2017. In part the military downsizing was due to budgetary constraints, in part to the end of the American combat missions in Iraq (December 2010) and Afghanistan (slated for December 2014). With fewer members of the armed forces, competition for the available positions can be expected to grow more intense.

One long-term trend in all the services is greater participation by women. The notion of the famale soldier, sailor, or marine assigned to duty at a telephone switchboard, nursing station, or file cabinet was discarded years ago. Today, women go through a basic training regimen that is just as rigorous as what their male counterparts experience. Until 2013, females in the U.S. armed services were officially barred from direct combat roles. Despite this policy, women routinely faced enemy fire—and in many cases were wounded or killed—in the wars in Afghanistan and Iraq, conflicts that didn't have traditional front lines. For example, the medic who jumped into the back of Jim Beverly's Humvee to administer first aid to the injured soldiers was a woman—Specialist Billie Grimes of Lebanon, Indiana. Grimes came under small-arms fire during the incident.

Like other women deployed in Iraq and Afghanistan, Grimes was "attached" rather than assigned to a combat infantry unit. But often that was a distinction without a difference. Secretary of Defense Leon Panetta acknowledged as much when, in early 2013, he rescinded the policy of prohibiting women from official combat roles. Panetta's decision was widely welcomed. "We're already here," noted Kelly Hasselman, an army captain commanding a company of female soldiers in Kandahar, Afghanistan. "It's just not officially been in the books." For his part, Hasselman's battalion commander, Lieutenant Colonel Thomas Anderson, said that gender wasn't an issue in a soldier's effectiveness. "Gender, height, weight, religion, sexual preference, race—I don't care," Anderson claimed. "It all comes down to your ability to do what the Army asks you to do."

However, some observers questioned the wisdom of opening up combat positions to women. Among the more outspoken of those critics was Bing West, a military historian, former assistant secretary of defense, and Vietnam veteran. West didn't doubt that some female warriors would excel in combat. "There are women with Olympic-standard physical, mental and psychological attributes who could lead a SEAL or Army Delta team," he wrote. "But they are as rare as Olympic athletes." In general, West asserted, women don't have the necessary strength or stamina to fight a prolonged ground war. If their representation in combat units were equivalent to their overall proportion of the active-duty armed forces—about 15 percent as of 2013—then in West's view the military might be courting disaster in the next big ground conflict. Time will tell whether such warnings are prescient or unfounded.

"I Want You"

Filling the ranks of America's all-volunteer military is a never-ending task. In a recent year the services combined had some 15,000 personnel assigned to the job of recruiting young people. It was estimated that the Department of Defense spent $11,000 to recruit each person it convinced to sign up for the military—for an annual total of about $2 billion.

Recruiting campaigns have come a long way since 1916, when artist James Montgomery Flagg painted an image of a stern-looking Uncle Sam pointing out toward the onlooker with the message "I Want You for the U.S. Army." The army printed more than 4 million of the posters in 1917 and 1918, using them as a recruiting tool during World War I. Now, recruiting campaigns are conceived by high-powered professional advertising agencies. They feature frequent use of television commercials and, in recent years, sponsorship of race cars and development of video games

I WANT YOU FOR U.S. ARMY

NEAREST RECRUITING STATION

designed to give a teenager a virtual taste of the exciting life in store for a member of the military.

In 2002, the army unveiled a video game titled *America's Army* and made it free online for downloading. Development cost of the game was reported at more than $6 million. Within the first year of its release, *America's Army* had been downloaded by more than 6 million users. Recruiters also distributed some 2.7 million free CD-R versions of the game to potential recruits. Clearly, the game was developed with a teenage audience in mind. Lieutenant Colonel Casey Wardynski, an economics teacher at the U.S. Military Academy at West Point, New York, told *Wired* magazine, "In World War II we had newsreels. Then came TV ads. More recently we've had banners. This is just the next step."

By playing *America's Army*, young people can obtain a virtual experience of basic training at Fort Benning, Georgia, complete with a run through an obstacle course, practice session on the target range, and a barking drill sergeant, who admonishes the recruits not to "mess up my freshly raked sand pit." Following graduation from basic training, players take part in team-oriented missions, which they can play online against other virtual soldiers. In one scenario, team members are given the job of defending the Alaska oil pipeline. Another scenario calls for them to rescue a soldier from terrorists hiding in the mountains. The game's designers concentrated on realism: players could experience the recoil from guns after they fired them, although users did notice that the violence seemed a bit sanitized.

The military is finding other ways to reach out to young people. In recent years, the service branches have sponsored entries on the NASCAR racing circuit, specifically targeting fans between the ages of 17 and 28. Also, the services sponsor drag racing teams on the NHRA circuit. "Because NASCAR and NHRA speak to the same markets we target, it was natural for us to follow," Captain Derek Campbell, a marketing initiatives officer for the U.S. Marines, told *USA Today*. "Having a car drives up the awareness of the Marine Corps. It drives up the number of contacts, and our hope is that it leads to [enlistment] contracts."

Chapter Five

Ralph Nader ran for president in 2000 as leader of the Green Party, and proved to be very popular among young people. When he announced an independent candidacy in 2004, he said that young volunteers would be even more important to his presidential campaign.

Teenagers Who Campaign: Making Their Voices Heard

In May 2000, Ralph Nader stood on a stage in Boston, Massachusetts, surrounded by teenagers who had just clamored to meet him following a speech he delivered in a city park. Nader was the presidential candidate of the Green Party, an organization composed mostly of young, dedicated advocates of environmental protection, consumer rights, and other populist ideals.

That year, none of the experts gave Nader and the Greens much chance to compete with the well-established Republican and Democratic parties in the national presidential election. As the campaign wore on, it became clear that while the Republicans and Democrats were relying on well-financed campaigns, TV advertising, and the efforts of both professional political consultants and party regulars, the Greens were fueled by little more than the determination of its candidate and his young, enthusiastic volunteers, most of whom were high school and college students.

The 2000 election would turn out to be the closest presidential race in U.S. history. Al Gore, at the time the vice president, would receive over half a million more popular votes than Republican nominee George W. Bush, but he would ultimately lose the elections. Presidential elections are decided in the Electoral College. Each state casts a certain number of votes in the Electoral College, based on the state's population; the candidate who gets the most popular votes in the state generally gets all of the state's electoral votes. To win the presidency, a candidate needs 270 electoral votes. On the day after the 2000 election, Gore had 266 electoral votes and Bush had 246. However, the vote in Florida, where 25 electoral votes were at stake, was so close that it had to be recounted. Both parties pushed for political advantage, and after more than a month of recounts, the U.S. Supreme Court declared that the recounts should end with Bush holding a 537-vote lead. Bush was awarded Florida's electoral votes, giving him 271 and the presidency.

Both Gore and Bush received more than 50 million votes; Nader finished a distant third with less than 3 million votes. Yet many people believe Nader cost Gore the election. The Democratic Party can usually count on support from environmental activists and others who oppose corporate influence in government, so if Nader had stayed out of the 2000 race, most of his supporters would probably have voted for Gore. More than 97,000 people voted for Nader in Florida; had even a small majority of them voted instead for Gore, he would have easily won Florida and the presidency.

However, the fact that a third-party candidate running an underfunded campaign convinced nearly 3 million Americans to vote for him illustrates the effectiveness of young people as a polit-

TEENS' VOTING ATTITUDES

		Won't vote if don't like candidates	Local elections are not important	Always vote along party lines
Gender	Male	30	20	16
	Female	27	19	12
Age	13 to 15	28	18	11
	16 to 17	29	22	18
Race	White	24	20	14
	Non-white	42	19	14
Educational Status	Above-average students	26	16	14
	Average and below	32	25	13
Economic Background	White collar	26	17	12
	Blue collar	31	19	13
Region	East	33	22	14
	Midwest	28	16	13
	South	22	15	14
	West	34	28	14
Political Affiliation	Republican	23	20	14
	Democrat	34	20	15

Poll taken October 1990; 500 total respondents.
Source: The Gallup Organization.

ical force. Without money to buy television advertisements or flood mailboxes with campaign literature, and shut out of nationally televised debates by the representatives of the established parties, Nader relied on thousands of teenage volunteers to walk their neighborhoods or stand on street corners, handing out information to voters. In cheap storefront offices or basements of private homes, Green Party volunteers called voters and asked them to consider their candidate. They posted signs in alleys of city neighborhoods, tacked posters to telephone poles in suburban housing developments, wrote letters to newspaper editors in small towns, and staged rallies on college campuses. "It is a shoestring operation," Gwen Marshall, head of Nader's campaign in Ohio told the *Cincinnati Enquirer*. "There is nothing high-powered about this. It is strictly grass-roots stuff."

An Extreme Example

The notion that young people can sway public policy by working for candidates is not new. In 1968, Democratic presidential candidate Eugene McCarthy received the overwhelming support of young people when he announced his opposition to the Vietnam War. McCarthy did not win the Democratic nomination, but his campaign would set the future anti-war tone for the Democratic Party.

During the late 1960s and early 1970s many draft-age men marched on college campuses, burned their draft cards, fled to Canada, or went to jail rather than submit to military service in Vietnam. Their opposition to the war influenced an incumbent president, Lyndon Johnson, not to run for a second term in 1968. As more people became convinced that the war was wrong, the politicians in power got the message and began to withdraw the troops. By 1973, all U.S. combat troops had been recalled from Southeast Asia.

Mobilizing opposition to the Vietnam War is an extreme example of how high school and college students have used their resources to sway public opinion. Often, the issues that draw young people to work for candidates are far less significant than the morality of a war. Young people may feel that laws are too intrusive and work to change their communities on a local level. For example, teenagers may fight to overturn local

Teenagers often become more involved in politics when they realize that political decisions will directly affect them. These Brooklyn students are protesting against the war in Iraq on March 5, 2003.

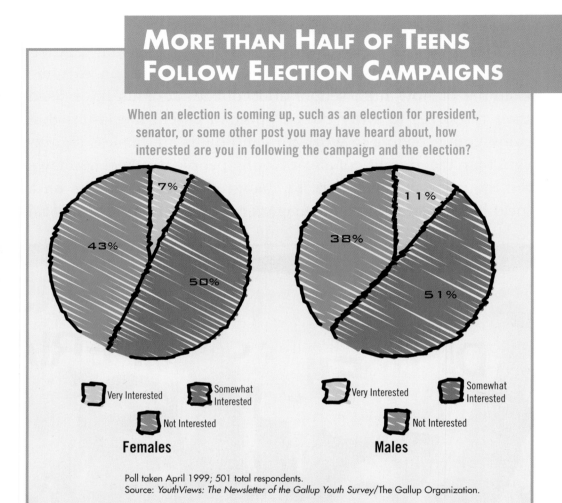

MORE THAN HALF OF TEENS FOLLOW ELECTION CAMPAIGNS

When an election is coming up, such as an election for president, senator, or some other post you may have heard about, how interested are you in following the campaign and the election?

Females

7%
43%
50%

Very Interested • Somewhat Interested • Not Interested

Males

11%
38%
51%

Very Interested • Somewhat Interested • Not Interested

Poll taken April 1999; 501 total respondents.
Source: *YouthViews: The Newsletter of the Gallup Youth Survey*/The Gallup Organization.

ordinances that directly affect them, such as a curfew or the closing of a public park. Perhaps a school board has infringed on students' rights and the students decide it is time to fight back, so they find a candidate who agrees with their side and they go to work for him or her.

Sometimes teenagers get involved in politics for the same reasons that adults get involved: they feel taxes may be too high. When teenagers begin driving, and filling up their gas tanks, they may notice that fuel taxes make up a large portion of what they are charged for a gallon of gas. Teenagers who start working at after-school or weekend jobs may for the first time notice a big difference between their hourly wage and their take-home pay, thanks to deductions for Social Security and other government programs.

"I encourage young people to get involved in politics," former vice presidential candidate Geraldine Ferraro said in an interview with PBS's *NewsHour*. "I believe as citizens they not only have the right to vote, but an obligation to learn the issues so that they vote intelligently. The best way to do that is to get involved in politics. I also believe that it is important that young people understand the power of public office to do good."

Paying Attention to the World

Young citizens have the right to vote once they are 18 years old, but history shows that comparatively few of them register, and of course not all of the young people who register to vote actually cast ballots. Tufts University political science professor James Glaser told CNN, "College students are the worst voters that are out there, mostly because they are highly mobile and they're new to the communities that they live in." In the 2000 presidential election, 76 percent of the registered voters of the United States went to the polls, but just 28 percent of the voters between the ages of 18 and 24 cast ballots in the election.

Voting is the most basic form of political activism that can be found in the United States. Why the reluctance by young people to get involved? The Washington-based American Political Science Association looked into that issue in a 2003 study. The association interviewed some 3,200 people between the ages of 15 and 25, and found that while a large number of youths perform ed volunteer work—largely the result of school-mandated compulsory community service requirements—few of them were drawn to politically oriented activities.

The association found that students most likely to volunteer for political campaigns were usually young people who were involved in their student governments. The involvement of those young people in politics tended to continue after they left high school. "Students who participate in political groups in high school continue to be disproportionately civically and politically active after graduation," said the study. "Among high school graduates, those who participated in political organizations while in school vote more frequently (38 percent vs. 21 percent), are more attentive to news (36 percent vs. 24 percent), and volunteer regularly at twice the rate (33 percent vs. 15 percent) as those without experience in those organizations. They are also more likely to give voice to their concerns through boycotting, signing petitions, or contacting public officials or the news media."

The study also found that parental influence had a lot to do with a teenager's political activism. The young people interviewed by the study's authors said they were more likely to vote and become politically active if their parents were willing to engage them in political dialogue at home.

In 1999, the Gallup Youth Survey found that a surprisingly large group of teenagers were not paying attention to the world around them. The survey found that 32 percent of the respondents could not identify Al Gore as the vice president. What's more, 84 percent of the young people who participated did not know the identity of the secretary of state—at the time, Madeleine Albright—and 94 percent could not name the chief justice of the U.S. Supreme Court, William Rehnquist.

A year later, the Gallup Youth Survey conducted a poll to gauge interest in the 2000 presidential election. The Gallup Organization interviewed 501 young people between the ages of 13 and 17 from January through April in 2000. At the time, fights were being waged for both the Republican and Democratic nominations for president. As such, political stories were in the news each day, the presidential election was undoubtedly being discussed in high school history and political science classes across the country, and parents debated the merits of the candidates across the dinner table. Yet the Gallup Youth Survey found that just 9 percent of the respondents were "very interested" in the presidential campaign.

The Importance of Young People

Although the number of young people who volunteer to work in political campaigns is small, teens who do become involved with political causes generally do so with great enthusiasm. During the 2000 election, one such volunteer was Anna Lyman, at the time a 16-year-old resident of Manchester, New Hampshire. Anna decided to work for Vice President Al Gore's campaign that year. Unlike many young volunteers, though, Anna found herself campaigning shoulder to shoulder with the candidate. She told *Upfront*, a publication of the New York Times, "[W]alking alongside [Gore] was really exciting. I helped direct him to the right houses; they were targeted Democratic houses, but were undecided in the primary. He knocked on the doors himself. I thought one woman was going to faint, she was so surprised — and very elated, too — to have him there."

Another New Hampshire teenager, 17-year-old Lee Herman, worked for the campaign of Republican candidate Steve Forbes.

"When voter turnout goes up, I believe it's because of volunteers like us," he told *Upfront*. "At rallies, we get out there and make some noise—we're having a good time. We come out and spread the word and get people to the polls. On primary day we're going to have people driving buses and cars, driving people to the polls who wouldn't be able to get there otherwise."

Four years later, candidates had come to realize the importance of young people to the electoral process. During the 2004 election, most of the major candidates reached out to youthful supporters. In November 2003, a year before the election, most of the candidates vying for the Democratic nomination participated in a debate specifically designed for a young audience. The debate was sponsored by CNN and MTV, and was part of the "Rock the Vote" campaign that had been founded by MTV more than a decade earlier. For the debate, most of the candidates dressed casually and reserved their comments for issues they believed would be of interest to the young audience. For example, candidates John Kerry, Howard Dean, and John Edwards admitted using marijuana as young men, while Dennis Kucinich told the audience that he believed marijuana should be legalized. Following the forum, Harvard University student Betsy Sykes told CNN, "I think the real message here is that the youth vote is up for grabs, and that we're not apathetic. We're not disengaged like everyone thinks we are."

Rock the Vote is one of several organizations that have been established to encourage young people to vote and otherwise become politically active. The Los Angeles-based organization stages concerts as well as rallies on college campuses. Many rock stars have endorsed the effort and can often be counted on to perform at a Rock the Vote event. Rock the Vote also helps put young people in touch with other organizations in need of volunteers and supporters. Many of those groups work to protect the environment. They include Greenpeace, the Sierra Club, and the Student Environmental Action Coalition. "The message we want to send to people is that if they want things to change they have to vote—if they don't vote, no one is going to listen to them," said Steve Guy, an MTV representative who spoke with

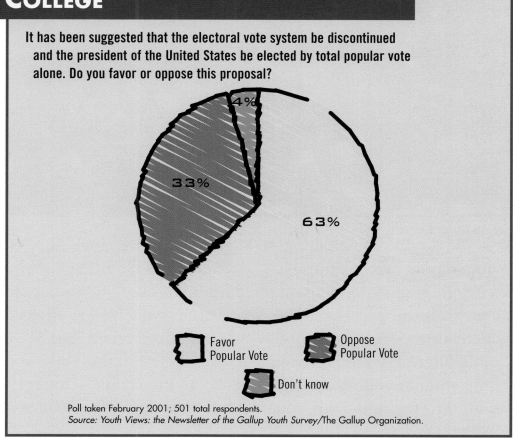

TEEN VIEWS ON THE ELECTORAL COLLEGE

It has been suggested that the electoral vote system be discontinued and the president of the United States be elected by total popular vote alone. Do you favor or oppose this proposal?

4%

33%

63%

Favor Popular Vote

Oppose Popular Vote

Don't know

Poll taken February 2001; 501 total respondents.
Source: Youth Views: the Newsletter of the Gallup Youth Survey/The Gallup Organization.

First Lady Michelle Obama speaks during a 2012 presidential campaign event at a middle school in Nevada. Young voters played a crucial role in the 2008 election of Barack Obama as president, and in his 2012 re-election.

the University of Washington's student newspaper shortly before a rally on the campus.

Another effort to increase the participation of young people in the political process is the nonpartisan New Voters Project, which is supported by George Washington University, the State Public Interest Research Groups, and the Pew Charitable Trusts. Using student volunteers, the New Voters Project seeks to register Americans and help ensure that they go to the polls on Election Day.

Young people played a vital role in the 2008 presidential election. The Democratic nominee, Barack Obama, was a U.S. senator from Illinois who, years earlier, had worked as a community organizer in Chicago. Obama's campaign built effective grassroots organizations all across the country, with enthusiastic young volunteers making up much of the workforce. The candidate's message of hope and political change resonated with young voters. Obama won two-thirds of the voters in the 18–29 age group, which helped seal his victory over Republican nominee John McCain. Nationwide, Obama won 52.9 percent of the popular vote to McCain's 45.6 percent.

In 2012, President Obama appeared to face long odds to win reelection. The U.S. economy, which had been in free fall when Obama took office in 2009, remained sluggish. Unemployment hovered around 8 percent. As in 2008, the Obama campaign targeted the youth vote, this time making especially savvy use of social media. The popular vote was closer than it had been in 2008, but Obama came out ahead, winning 51 percent to Republican challenger Mitt Romney's 47.2 percent. Again, Obama won two-thirds of the youth vote, which proved decisive.

Chapter Six

Young people march in New York City as part of an Occupy Wall Street demonstration, December 2011. Occupy Wall Street was meant to draw attention to corruption in the U.S. financial system, as well as to the undue influence of the "wealthiest 1 percent" in American politics.

When Volunteerism Turns to Activism

Although many teenagers supported the war in Iraq and believed military service is important to keep America strong, a vocal anti-war movement also made itself heard in the months leading up the invasion. Many of the loudest critics of the war were young people. In the San Francisco area, for example, many high school students walked out of classes in the spring of 2003 to protest the war. Their walkout was organized by the National Youth and Student Peace Coalition, a network of groups that formed following the 2001 terrorist attacks and the subsequent U.S.-led invasion of Afghanistan.

One student who told a reporter for the *San Jose Mercury* News that she planned to participate in the walkout was Rachelle Cruz, 17, who attended Tennyson High School in Hayward, California. Cruz said she realized that walking out of classes was against school rules and that she faced a possible suspension. Nevertheless, the young activist said, she believed that participating in the protest was important to send a message to authorities that all young people did not support the war. Cruz said she could endure whatever punishment she faced at school. "We're worried that we might get suspended, but then all of these people could die in Iraq so we're trying to keep it in perspective," said Cruz, who volunteered to help organize the walkout by circulating fliers announcing the protest and contacting students at other schools.

Elsewhere, teenagers found ways to participate in other anti-war protests. At another anti-war protest in San Francisco, attended by some 150,000 people, a group of students from the College of Marin made the trip to the city in a crowded bus that left the campus in the early morning hours. Most of them were forced to stand for the entire trip. In Portsmouth, New Hampshire, many teenagers were among the 100 people who attended an anti-war rally in the town's Market Square. They carried signs that read, "What would Jesus do? No war for oil!" And in Southern California, 25 students staged a walkout from Temescal Canyon High School in Riverside, then stood in the rain to protest the coming invasion of Iraq. The protest was organized by the members of the school's Peace Club. During the protest, students held signs that read "No War" and "Don't Invade Iraq." Peace Club president Ted Hemmings, 16, told a reporter for the *Riverside Press-Enterprise*, "We're trying to reach people who think war is the only solution. We need outdoor rallies to let all people know this." Hemmings carried a sign that read, "What would Gandhi do?"

Protests by Young People

For teenagers, volunteerism doesn't necessarily mean filing papers in a hospital office, sorting through second-hand clothes in a homeless shelter, or stuffing envelopes at campaign headquarters. Many young people volunteer their time and talents for causes that are not organized by established charitable groups. Instead of working in the back of an ambulance, they carry picket signs. Instead of teaching inner-city children how to read, they hand out pamphlets at an anti-nuclear power demonstration. Instead of volunteering for the U.S. Army, they lead anti-war protests.

Whatever cause interests them, chances are their activities will be spontaneous, full of energy, originality, and carried out with a feeling that comes from deep within their souls. They have decided that something is wrong, they refuse to be a part of it, and they intend to do what they can to make it right. Whatever these young people decide to do, their activities will often be designed to send

Philadelphia students participate in a "Die-In" on the steps of City Hall to protest the war in Iraq.

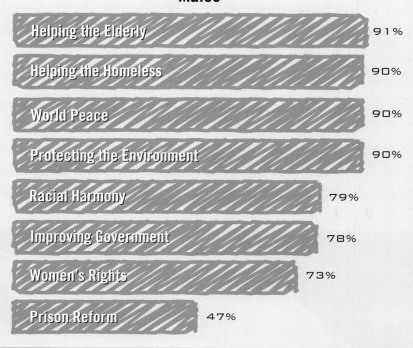

CAUSES TEENS ARE WILLING TO SERVE

Males

Helping the Elderly	91%
Helping the Homeless	90%
World Peace	90%
Protecting the Environment	90%
Racial Harmony	79%
Improving Government	78%
Women's Rights	73%
Prison Reform	47%

the government or another figure in authority a very direct and not-too-subtle message.

Sometimes, the activities of young protesters can be quite theatrical, intended to capture the attention of news reporters and camera crews covering the event. For example, in November 2003 some 10,000 demonstrators, many of whom were students, gathered outside the gates of Fort Benning. This military post in Georgia is the home of the Western Hemispheric Institute for Security Cooperation, a school where the U.S. Army trains military personnel from Latin American countries. The protesters

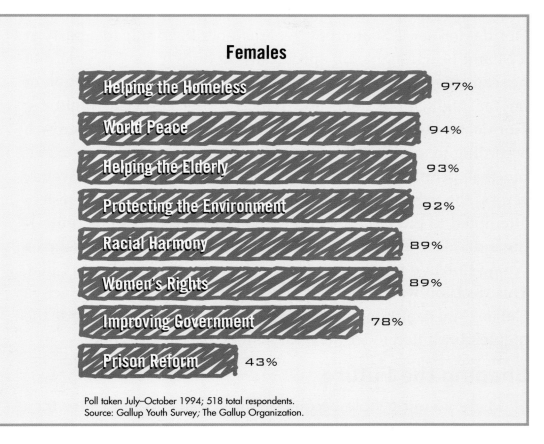

Females

Helping the Homeless	97%
World Peace	94%
Helping the Elderly	93%
Protecting the Environment	92%
Racial Harmony	89%
Women's Rights	89%
Improving Government	78%
Prison Reform	43%

Poll taken July–October 1994; 518 total respondents.
Source: Gallup Youth Survey; The Gallup Organization.

complained that some of the graduates of the school use the training in tactics and strategy they obtain at Fort Benning to abuse the citizens of their own countries. For example, protesters said, some years ago six Jesuit priests, a worker, and a teenage girl in El Salvador were killed by soldiers who had attended the Fort Benning school. As part of their protest, they held a mock funeral for the victims, marching in a procession in which black-cloaked volunteers carried eight cardboard coffins to symbolize the fate of the victims. The protesters demanded that the school be closed down.

Sometimes, protesters can show up when the establishment least expects it. In 2002, while campaigning for governor of Florida, former U.S. attorney general Janet Reno staged a party at a Miami Beach nightclub specifically to draw young people into her campaign. To the delight of her many supporters, Reno got up on the nightclub's stage and danced. "It's a special night for Florida, for Dade County and for the nation," Reno told the crowd, according to a story published in the *Miami Herald*. "It's an example that people can come together, young and old." However, across the street from the nightclub, five teenage protesters attempted to put a damper on the party. They held signs protesting a decision Reno had made while attorney general to return a young Cuban refugee named Elian Gonzalez to his father in Cuba. This decision was bitterly opposed in Florida's politically active Cuban-American community, and the teens who stood outside the nightclub wanted to let Reno know they had not forgotten.

Shaping the Future

Many young people become dedicated activists because they believe their efforts can make a difference. In 1991, a Gallup Youth Survey found that teens favored community action to improve conditions in society. A total of 78 percent of boys and 86 percent of girls who responded to the poll said they favored community action. Another 1991 poll found that 19 percent of the respondents said they would participate in protests while 15 percent said they would join boycotts. In 1999, the Gallup Youth Survey posed a number of questions to young people between the ages of 13 and 17 to gauge the roles teens felt they would play in shaping the future. A total of 78 percent of the respondents said they would "definitely" or "probably" contribute to a society that is less likely to discriminate against people on the basis of their race. Also, 73 percent of the respondents said they would help provide a new hope and sense of purpose for the world. Eighty-one percent of the teens who participated in the poll said they would contribute to a world that would be less likely to discriminate against women, while 79 percent of the respondents said they hoped to be part of a society that would be more concerned about people who are less fortunate. Also in the survey, 75 percent of the teens said they hoped to contribute to a society that is less likely to discriminate against gays or single parents, 67 percent said they hoped to contribute to a world that is less polluted and more caring about the environment, and 66 percent said they hoped to shape a future that would see fewer wars and armed conflicts.

With these high levels of interest, it is no wonder that when the government disappoints or enrages teenagers by relaxing standards against polluters, or passes a law deemed to be anti-gay, or cuts off assistance to poor people, young activists are often inspired to pick up a picket sign to let the government know how they feel.

It is unfair, though, to say all protests are aimed at the government or people in authority. In New York City's tough South Bronx neighborhood, a group of teenagers led a protest against drug dealers who took over a city park. One of the leaders of the "Take Back the Park" movement was 17-year-old Gabby Bernardez, a leader of an organization known as Youth Force. Bernardez's group organized a series of events to protest the drug dealers. One event drew 1,000 people. Soon, Youth Force took its anti-drug activism to other neighborhoods. "We came from the same kinds of neighborhoods as the kids we're helping," Bernardez told *Upfront*. "We try to show them that if we can do it, they can do it too."

Although protests draw attention, voting is the most powerful way to affect national politics. In 1971, the legal voting age was lowered from 21 to 18 years of age; some people would like to see the age lowered to 16 or 17.

Not all activism takes the shape of public protests, either. Sometimes, more conventional methods are employed, such as working through the court system to change laws. In Anchorage, Alaska, three teenagers sued the city government to overturn an ordinance establishing a curfew of 11 P.M. for people under the age of 18. Teenagers Brenna Riordan, David Treacy, and Sam Williford enlisted the Alaska chapter of the American Civil Liberties Union (ACLU) to file the legal challenge. One of the plaintiffs in the case said he was cited while driving home from a friend's house at 2 A.M. The teenager said he had planned to stay at his friend's home overnight, but became ill and decided to drive the two miles home. The teenager claimed that he called ahead to his mother first, who gave him permission to drive home. ACLU head

Jennifer Rudinger was quoted on the Alaskan Libertarian Party's Internet page as saying, "There are countless instances in which fairness and justice dictate that teens should be allowed to travel at night. No city council could possibly foresee every instance in which it would be good public policy to allow an exception to the curfew law. Therefore, parents should be empowered to make these decisions, since governments cannot."

Changing the Voting Age

In recent years, many young American activists have been agitating for the government to lower the voting age to 16 or 17. Lowering the voting age would require an amendment to the U.S. Constitution, an action that would have to be approved by Congress as well as by two-thirds of all state legislatures. That is what occurred in 1971, when the voting age was lowered from 21 to 18. At the time, veterans returning from the Vietnam War, many of whom were under 21, demanded the right to vote. They argued that if they were young enough to be drafted it was wrong to deny them the right to vote. Government leaders were hard-pressed to turn them down, and the right of 18-year-old citizens to vote sailed through the state legislatures and was quickly adopted as the Twenty-sixth Amendment to the Constitution.

These days, there seems to be little interest in Congress or many of the state legislatures to lower the voting age. Many 16- and 17-year-old teens themselves have said they doubt whether they would vote, even if given the opportunity. For example, in a 1991 Gallup Youth Survey, 29 percent of 16- and 17-year-olds said they would not vote if they did not like the candidates, and another 22 percent said they did not think local elections were important.

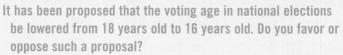

TEEN VIEWS ON LOWERING THE VOTING AGE

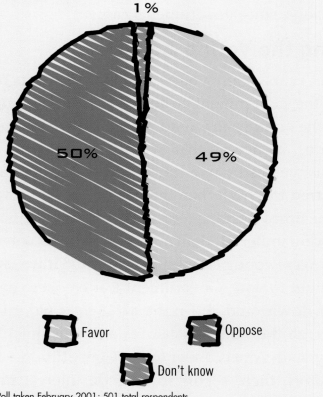

It has been proposed that the voting age in national elections be lowered from 18 years old to 16 years old. Do you favor or oppose such a proposal?

1%

50%   49%

☐ Favor   ☐ Oppose

☐ Don't know

Poll taken February 2001; 501 total respondents.
Source: Youth Views: the Newsletter of the Gallup Youth Survey/The Gallup Organization.

Yet, teenagers in many cities are agitating for the voting age to be lowered. Active campaigns are under way in Florida, Hawaii, North Dakota, Alaska, and New York. "Young people have jobs, pay taxes, go to school to learn about government, and know the issues," teenage voting rights activist Laura

Finstad told ABC News. "We think 16 would be a fair age to be able to vote."

The activists have met with some success. In Cambridge, Massachusetts, the city council approved lowering the voting age to 17 for city elections. But for the measure to go into effect, it would need the approval of the Massachusetts legislature. As of early 2013, state lawmakers had declined to take up the issue. Legislative committees in Maine, Texas, California, and Minnesota have staged debate on lowering the voting age. In Washington, D.C., the National Youth Rights Association has also embraced the cause of lowering the voting age. Although the organization does not regard itself solely as an activist organization, members of the group have led protests and other public demonstrations to call attention to their demands.

Chapter Seven

A college student speaks with an elderly woman at a Connecticut nursing home as part of an oral history project. By volunteering, young people have a chance to really make a difference in their communities, learn about the past, and make new friends.

Teens Who Make a Difference

When Emily Douglas was 10 years old, she accompanied her mother to the supermarket on the night before Thanksgiving to pick up some last-minute groceries for the next evening's feast. On the way out of the store, Emily couldn't help but notice a young girl and her mother waiting in the checkout line. While most everyone else in line had turkeys and Thanksgiving dinner trimmings in their shopping carts, Emily saw the girl and her mother were buying bread and bologna. "Why don't they have a turkey like us?" Emily asked her mother.

"Not everyone is as fortunate as us," Emily's mother replied. "Your grandmother grew up like that." Emily, who later described her experience in *Angels on Earth* magazine, noted that her grandmother had just died. Emily recalled how much her grandmother had enjoyed holidays: preparing meals and making sure all her grandchildren had presents for Christmas. "Every kid should have a

Christmas," Emily's grandmother would tell people.

At that point, Emily resolved to dedicate her life to her grandmother's spirit. The young girl from Powell, Ohio, founded

RESOURCES FOR TEEN VOLUNTEERS

As the examples in this chapter illustrate, young people don't need much other than their own resources and energy to become effective volunteers. Other teenagers may want to make use of established organizations to help them make decisions on the best ways to help others.

Young people interested in joining AmeriCorps can contact the organization through its Web page or by getting in touch with the Corporation for National and Community Service in Washington, DC.

Young people over the age of 17 who want to find out about enlisting in the military need only visit their local recruiters. The army, navy, air force and marines all maintain recruiting offices in most American communities. Representatives from the services usually maintain booths or tables at career fairs. Two Internet pages that provide information about volunteering for the armed services are http://www.usmilitary.about.com and http://www.military.com.

The Peace Corps can be contacted through its website at http://www.peacecorps.gov, or by calling 1-855-855-1961 for the address of a regional recruiting office.

Volunteers of America provides services in about 300 American communities. To find a local office, visit http://www.voa.org/Local-Offices.

A national organization that makes use of more than 1 million volunteers is the American Red Cross, 2025 E Street NW, Washington, DC, 20006. The phone number is 1-800-733-2767. The Internet address is http://www.redcross.org. People can donate their time to

Grandma's Gifts, which raises money for food, clothes, and toys for poor children growing up in the Appalachian region in Ohio, Kentucky, and West Virginia. To launch the program, Emily wrote to family members and others for donations. Other donors signed on. By the time she was 19 years old, Emily found herself at the

the Red Cross and they can donate their money. The Red Cross also asks for donations of blood, which it supplies to hospitals throughout the United States.

Goodwill Industries International Inc. operates some 1,900 retail stores where donated clothing and household goods are sold to support Goodwill's many charitable efforts. As such, the organization is in need of a lot of help from volunteers. People willing to donate their time can find their local Goodwill chapter by checking http://www.goodwill.org/uncategorized/faqs.

Habitat for Humanity International, which builds homes for low-income people using donated materials and volunteer labor, has many campus chapters and youth programs, not all of which require young people to help build homes. Youths are encouraged to partici-pate in HabiFest, an annual day of rallies and other activities calling for government support of affordable housing. Local chapters can be found at the organization's website at http://www.habitat.org, or by contacting Habitat for Humanity at its headquarters, located at 121 Habitat Street, Americus, GA, 31709-3498. The phone number is 1-800-HABITAT.

head of an organization that had raised more than $1 million in contributions and supplied food, clothing, toys, and books to some 3,000 children.

When it comes to volunteering, some young people see a need in their community that is not being met by a government agency or social services program. They become leaders, doing what it takes to raise money, recruit other volunteers, and establish programs to help people in need. Despite commitments to schoolwork and extracurricular activities, these teenagers are somehow able to find the time and resources to accomplish what well-established community aid programs have managed to neglect.

In Miami, Florida, for example, 17-year-old Seraphin Bernard saw that young children in his neighborhood were not being taught art in their schools. So Seraphin started an art class for low-income children, paying for the art supplies out of his own pocket. Soon, the honors student was also leading classes in photography as well. "My payment is my students' smiles," he told a reporter for *Parade* magazine. "Nothing brings me more happiness than knowing I'm making a positive impact on people."

True Liberty

In 2003, the Gallup Youth Survey asked 517 young people between the ages of 13 and 17 to comment on their goals in life. As expected, a large majority of the respondents said their goals included finishing high school, attending college, and getting a good job. Many teens also said they wanted to marry, raise a family, and be financially secure. Five percent of the respondents, though, said their goal in life was to "make a difference" by helping people.

Laura-Beth Moore is someone who has made a difference in Houston, Texas. When Laura-Beth was 12 years old, she attended a recycling demonstration during an Earth Day program. Afterward, she discovered that her city did not provide curbside recycling for its citizens. This meant people in Houston threw away old newspapers, glass, plastic bottles, and aluminum cans. Laura-Beth wrote a letter to the mayor of Houston asking the city to start a curbside recycling program. She received a polite letter in return, advising her that no such program was in the city's plans. Not to be dissuaded, Laura-Beth spent her summer trying to start a curbside recycling program on her own. When she spoke publicly about her idea before a homeowners' association, a local legislator was in the audience. He backed the plan, and soon a local elementary school was serving as headquarters for a drop-off recycling center. People would deliver their recyclables to the school, where volunteers recruited by Laura-Beth separated the items and loaded them into trucks, to be driven to local recycling centers.

The first truck was actually rented with Laura-Beth's allowance money, but soon the program was earning enough money from the sale of recyclables to cover the cost of the trucks. Eventually, Laura-Beth's neighborhood program was collecting 20 tons of paper, glass, plastic, and metal a month. That prompted the city to take over the collection. It also prompted the city government to think again about curbside recycling and to include Laura-Beth in its plans. When she was 15 years old, Laura-Beth Moore was appointed to a seat on the board overseeing the Houston Waste Department.

Another teenager who spent a summer working for a cause was Celeste Lopez of Mesa, Arizona. As a young girl Celeste learned a lot about volunteering when she would tag along with her parents, who took meals to the migrant workers picking oranges in the fruit

The story of Laura-Beth Moore shows that one volunteer really can make a difference. As a 12-year-old she was started a recycling program that eventually took hold in an entire city.

groves outside Mesa. As she grew older, Celeste became more active, working in soup kitchens and helping to find apartments, health care, and jobs for homeless people in the Phoenix, Arizona, area. In high school, Celeste worked on her school paper, and she eventually decided to publish a newspaper for homeless people. The publication would give poor but talented writers and artists an outlet for their voices while at the same time providing news that the homeless population would find valuable. The first issue of *True Liberty*, a quarterly publication, was launched on July 4, 1997. Many of the poor people of the Phoenix area pitched in to help sell advertising or copies of the publication. Laura paid them a commission when they made a sale.

Eager to Affect Change

Anisa Kintz of Conway, South Carolina is the youngest person to address a United Nations forum. When she was 12 years old, Anisa was invited to speak before a UN conference on non-governmental organizations. Anisa had helped to start "Calling All Colors," a conference at Coastal Carolina University in which young people could share ideas about racial harmony.

Anisa conceived the idea for the conference during a volatile period in Conway. The community suffered from racial unrest after a black football player was suspended from the Conway High School team in 1991. Anisa approached university officials with the idea that a conference should be convened so that children could offer ideas on how people from different races might learn to live together. "After all," Anisa told the university magazine, "children are the future and new attitudes should start with us."

"Anisa's idea was, of course, exactly right," recalled Sally Hare, who at the time was Coastal Carolina's dean of graduate and continuing education. "We talked about the possibility of putting on a race awareness conference exclusively for children, but I felt that, in order for it to have its fullest possible effect and for it to be true to its purpose, the children would have to organize it and be responsible for it in every way possible. Anisa agreed."

Anisa recruited eight of her classmates to help plan the conference, which was attended by students in the third through eighth grades. During the conference, students met and talked about racial harmony. They played roles in skits and learned songs and dances together. More than 200 students from 20 schools attended the event. "Calling All Colors represents such a pure, pure thing in my life," said Allen Lee, who attended the conference. "It was such a frustrating time in Conway back then. For me, Calling All Colors became a 'safe spot.' At that first conference, I felt an absence of conflict that was refreshing and inspiring." Another student who attended, Stephen Garrett, said, "It was so much bigger than we realized at the time. The idea of making friends with kids of other races — and encouraging other kids to do the same — seems so simple, but it was really profound."

The first conference drew national news coverage. Soon, other schools held their own Calling All Colors conferences. As for Anisa Kintz, she became something of a celebrity. She was selected as one of President George H.W. Bush's "Thousand Points of Light," by the foundation he established to recognize contributions by volunteers. She also participated in the 1997 Summit for America's Future chaired by President Bill Clinton and future secretary of state Colin Powell in Philadelphia, and was asked to address the United Nations forum. Anisa, who went on to attend Macalester College in Minnesota, was for a time concerned that the attention lavished on her was drawing interest away from the true mission of Calling All Colors. Finally, though, Anisa said she decided, "If the program needs a symbol, I can be that symbol if necessary. The important thing is to recapture and sustain that childhood idealism. Now that we've grown up we should be more able and more eager to affect change."

Other Teens Who Make a Difference

Brutus and Ursula were orphaned black bear cubs captured in the wild. Brutus grew into a 400-pound adult bear while his sister Ursula tipped the scales at 300 pounds. Unfortunately, their accommodations at the zoo in California where they lived hardly met their needs. For 20 years, the two bears were forced to share a small cage. When it rained heavily, zookeepers had to move Brutus and Ursula to an even smaller cage because their regular cage tended to flood. Before moving the bears, zookeepers shot the animals with tranquilizers to ensure that they would be docile for the transfer.

When 13-year-old Justin Barker of Elk Grove, California, heard about the bears' living conditions, he decided to help. Justin formed the group Citizens Lobbying for Animals in Zoos, and started a campaign to raise money for a new home for Brutus and Ursula. It took four years, but Justin managed to raise $30,000 on his own while convincing private and corporate donors to contribute another $357,000. That money enabled the Folsom Zoo Sanctuary in California to erect a proper bear habitat for Brutus and Ursula. The bears' new home contained an air-conditioned sleeping den, a warm pool, trees, grass, and large boulders for climbing. After leading the fundraising campaign for the two bears, Justin said he intended to turn his attention to other animals

in need. He told *Animal Sheltering* magazine, "Helping captive wild animals in zoos and circuses is my passion in life."

Amondo Redmond grew up in a tough, crime-ridden neighborhood in Flint, Michigan. When he was 6 years old, his uncle was shot and killed. When Amondo was 14, he learned his cousin was killed in a drive-by shooting. That's when Amondo decided to get personally involved. He wrote to the mayor of Flint and asked him to establish a community violence protection program. The mayor liked the idea so much that he appointed Amondo county organizer for the effort, which was named the Youth Violence Prevention Coalition. Under Amondo's leadership, the coalition staged an annual Peaceful Solutions Rally, as well as dances and basketball games to keep teenagers off the streets. Amondo visited high schools in Flint to organize workshops on how to use peaceful means to resolve disputes. Authorities in Flint attributed a dramatic drop in crime by teenagers to the work undertaken by Amondo and others in the coalition.

Amondo's volunteerism didn't end after he left high school in Flint. An honors student, Amondo was flooded with college scholarships that totaled some $100,000. He elected to attend Michigan State University, which meant that he had far more money than he needed to obtain his college degree. So Amondo decided to establish a scholarship fund of his own, giving away portions of his own college money to other needy students. In an interview with Michigan State's student newspaper, Amondo said, "I hear a lot of students saying they have to leave school for financial reasons. I can help someone, so that's why I decided to do this."

Of course, teens like Amondo Redmond, Justin Barker, and Celeste Lopez are special people, but so are the many other teenagers whose stories were told in this book. In their own ways, each has captured the spirit of volunteerism, answering a call to duty that has found them helping to shelter the homeless, making a park a little cleaner, bandaging the wound of an injured motorist, or protecting America's freedom in a far-off land. Perhaps 16-year-old Jon Stiles of Newfound, New Hampshire, could be speaking for all teens who volunteer when he told *Baptist Standard* magazine why he spent his summers fixing up rundown houses. "When I help someone, something inside me happens," Jon said. "I don't know how to explain it, but my body literally changes. It feels so good."

Glossary

ABOLITIONIST—someone who works toward ending, or abolishing, slavery.

AMBASSADOR—a representative of an organization whose stature lends credibility to the group.

CARDIOPULMONARY RESUSCITATION (CPR)—a medical procedure used to restart a stopped heart.

COMMISSION—a percentage of a sale that is paid to the salesperson.

DRAFTEE—a person who is conscripted for military service.

ELECTORAL COLLEGE—the formal body elected by voters to choose the president and vice president of the United States.

EMPATHY—a feeling of care, often toward one who is less fortunate.

FLIERS—printed leaflets, usually distributed by hand in large numbers.

HALFWAY HOUSE—a place for formerly institutionalized people, such as released prisoners or recovering drug addicts, intended to facilitate their return to private life.

HUMANITARIAN—involving promotion of human welfare and social development.

INSURGENT—someone who rebels against authority or the government of a country.

MANDATORY—an activity that is required.

MIGRANT—a person who moves from location to location, often in search of work.

OBSTETRICS-GYNECOLOGY—a branch of medicine concerned with female reproductive organs and the fetal development and delivery of babies.

OBJECTIVISM—a philosophy espoused by the writer Ayn Rand, which emphasizes the superiority of individual accomplishments over those of the state or of society in general.

Glossary

ORDINANCE—a law or rule made by a city council or other governing body.

SHRAPNEL—small fragments of metal contained in a bomb that are released during the explosion so that they may fly out in many directions, causing injury or death to nearby victims.

TENET—a belief held to be true.

VALEDICTORIAN—the top student in a graduating class.

VOLUNTEERISM—the practice of using volunteer workers in community service organizations and programs.

Internet Resources

http://www.gallup.com

The home page of the Gallup Organization.

http://www.studentpirgs.org/campaigns/sp/new-voters-project

The mission of the New Voters Project is explained at this Internet site. Visitors can also find statistics and studies on the participation of young people in the political process, read press releases about the organization's activities, and find a list of contacts and instructions for getting involved.

http://www.rockthevote.org

Rock the Vote's activities are outlined on the organization's Web site. Visitors can find a calendar of events, list of celebrities and others supporting the effort, and position statements on a number of issues affecting young people, including the environment, free expression, violence, education, the economy, and the national debt. Also available are contacts for groups in need of volunteers.

http://www.youthrights.org

The website of the National Youth Rights Association includes essays on the organization's positions on many issues, including the drive to lower the voting age. Visitors will also find a calendar of events, speeches by NYRA leaders, and links to the association's local chapters, which have been established in New Hampshire, New York, Maryland, Virginia, North Carolina, Tennessee, Georgia, Massachusetts, Missouri, Wisconsin, North Dakota, California, and Washington, DC.

Internet Resources

http://www.unitedway.org/take-action/youth-volunteering
A page on youth and volunteering, from the nonprofit organization United Way.

http://www.unv.org/what-we-do/thematic-areas/youth.html
News, information, and reports about United Nations efforts to promote youth volunteerism across the world.

http://www.volunteerspot.com
This website helps people mobilize and coordinate volunteers in their communities. It is especially helpful for teachers.

Further Reading

Blaustein, Arthur I. *Make a Difference: Your Guide to Volunteering and Community Service.* Berkeley, Calif: Heyday Books, 2002.

Boyers, Sara Jane. *Teen Power Politics.* Brookfield, Conn.: Twenty-First Century Books, 2000.

Clark, Sondra. *77 Creative Ways Kids can Serve.* Indianapolis: Wesleyan Publishing House, 2008.

Friedman, Jenny, and Jolene Roehlkepartain. *Doing Good Together: 101 Easy, Meaningful Service Projects for Families, Schools, and Communities.* Minneapolis: Free Spirit, 2010.

Lewis, Barbara A. *The Teen Guide to Global Action: How to Connect with Others Near and Far to Create Social Change.* Minneapolis: Free Spirit, 2008.

Kayne, Sheryl. *Volunteer Vacations Across America.* Woodstock, Vt.: The Countryman Press, 2009.

McAdam, Doug, and Cynthia Brandt. *Assessing the Effects of Voluntary Youth Service: The Case of Teach for America.* Chapel Hill: University of North Carolina Press, 2010.

Index

Numbers in **bold italic** refer to captions and graphs.

Index

Index

Index

Index

Contributors

GEORGE GALLUP JR. (1930–2011) was involved with The Gallup Organization for more than 50 years. He served as chairman of The George H. Gallup International Institute and served on many boards involved with health, education, and religion, including the Princeton Religion Research Center, which he co-founded.

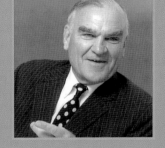

Mr. Gallup was internationally recognized for his research and study on youth, health, religion, and urban problems. He wrote numerous books, including *My Kids On Drugs?* with Art Linkletter (Standard, 1981); *The Great American Success Story* with Alec Gallup and William Proctor (Dow Jones-Irwin, 1986); *Growing Up Scared in America* with Wendy Plump (Morehouse, 1995); *Surveying the Religious Landscape: Trends in U.S. Beliefs* with D. Michael Lindsay (Morehouse, 1999); and *The Next American Spirituality* with Timothy Jones (Chariot Victor Publishing, 2002).

Mr. Gallup received his BA degree from the Princeton University Department of Religion in 1954, and held seven honorary degrees. He received many awards, including the Charles E. Wilson Award in 1994, the Judge Issacs Lifetime Achievement Award in 1996, and the Bethune-DuBois Institute Award in 2000. Mr. Gallup passed away in November 2011.

THE GALLUP YOUTH SURVEY was founded in 1977 by Dr. George Gallup to provide ongoing information on the opinions, beliefs and activities of America's high school students and to help society meet its responsibility to youth. The topics examined by the Gallup Youth Survey have covered a wide range—from abortion to zoology. From its founding through the year 2001, the Gallup Youth Survey sent more than 1,200 weekly reports to the Associated Press, to be distributed to newspapers around the nation.

HAL MARCOVITZ is a Pennsylvania-based journalist. He has written more than 50 books for young readers. His other titles for the Gallup Youth Survey series include *Teens and Career Choices* and *Teens and Volunteerism*. He lives in Chalfont, Pennsylvania, with his wife, Gail, and daughters Ashley and Michelle.